Embroidered
KITCHEN GARDEN

Embroidered Kitchen Garden
Published in 2019 by Zakka Workshop, a division of World Book Media, LLC

www.zakkaworkshop.com
134 Federal Street, 3rd Floor
Salem, MA 01970 USA
info@zakkaworkshop.com

KAZUKO AOKI'S EMBROIDERED KITCHEN GARDEN
All rights reserved. Copyright © 2017 Kazuko Aoki

Original Japanese edition published by
EDUCATIONAL FOUNDATION BUNKA GAKUEN BUNKA PUBLISHING BUREAU
English translation rights arranged through The English Agency (Japan) Ltd.
English language rights, translation & production by World Book Media, LLC

Publisher: Sunao Onuma
Author: Kazuko Aoki
Book Design: Mihoko Amano
Photography: Josui Yasuda (Bunka Publishing Bureau)
Trace: day studio Satomi Dairaku
DTP Operation: Bunka Phototype
Cooperation: Akiko Seino
Proofreading: Emiko Horiguchi
Editing: Yoko Osawa (Bunka Publishing Bureau)
Translator: Kristen Wolter
English Editor: Lindsay Fair
Designer: Nicola DosSantos

We have made every effort to ensure the accuracy and completeness of these instructions. We cannot, however, be responsible for human error, typographical mistakes, or variations in individual work.

ISBN: 978-1-940552-40-8

Printed in China

10 9 8 7 6 5 4 3 2 1

Embroidered
KITCHEN GARDEN

Vegetable, Herb & Flower Motifs to Stitch & Savor

KAZUKO AOKI

INTRODUCTION

My inspiration for this book was a cardboard box full of vegetables, fragrant with the aroma of the soil from a summer field.

Out of that box came brilliantly colored tomatoes in shapes I had never seen before, long, slender eggplants, beans in shades of purple and cream that I had never tasted, and leafy vegetables whose names I didn't even know.

I stilled the urge to taste them right away and began to sketch. In tomatoes patterned with red and green, there were also places where red mixed with purple. The white mottling of the zucchini was difficult to capture in watercolors. As I drew, I thought this might actually be easier to express in thread, and I began to feel like I was embroidering on the page.

The fresh combinations of vegetable colors and shapes are different from those of flowers, and after you are done sketching, you can enjoy their flavors as well. Sketching or embroidering the plants that surround you everyday will bring you closer to them.

Please enjoy this special time with vegetables as you work through the *Embroidered Kitchen Garden*.

—Kazuko Aoki

CONTENTS

KITCHEN GARDEN PLANNING

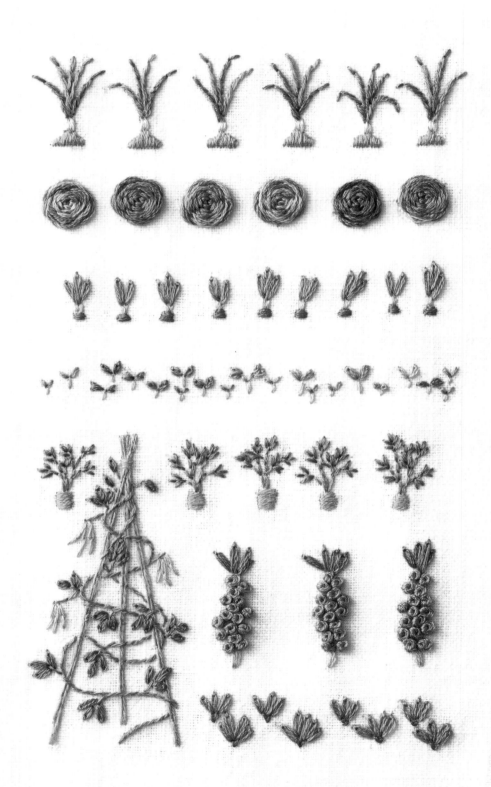

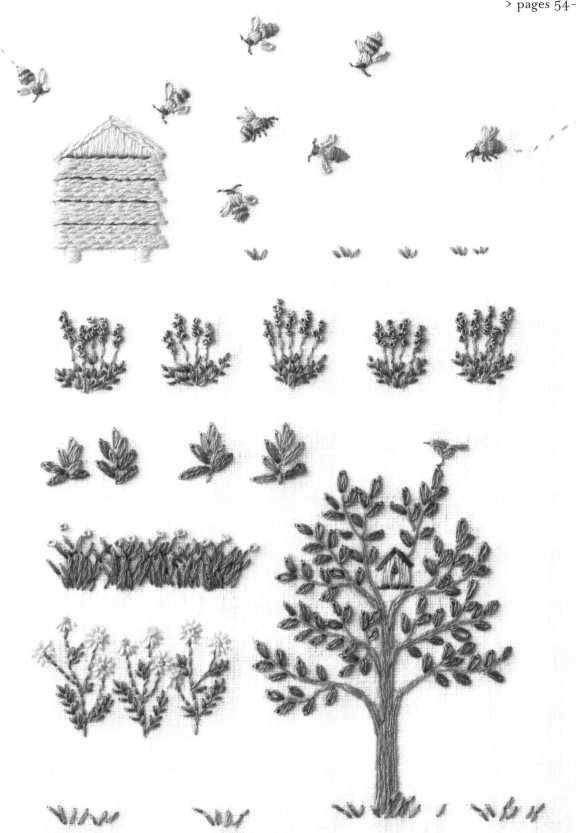

Tomatoes grow in an array of sizes and vivid colors. You will surely find a variety with the sweetness, tartness, and firmness you prefer.

> pages 56-57

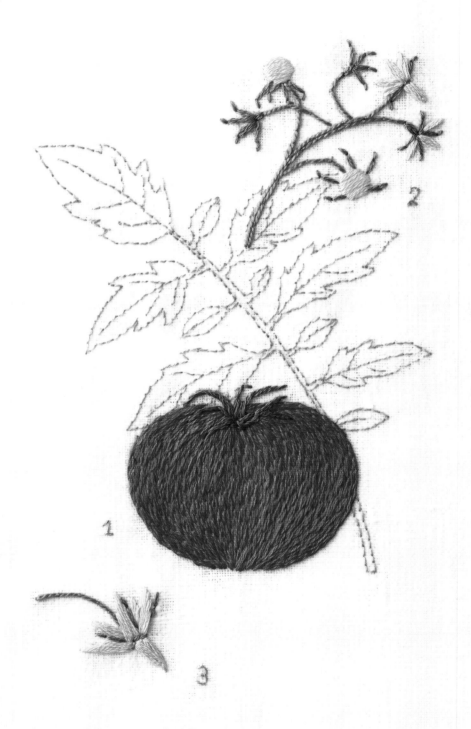

Tomato

'Sicilian Rouge'

'Aiko'

'Green Zebra'

'White Queen'

'Blackcherry'

'Tomatoberry'

Garden peas are a favorite companion plant for rambling roses. Both are wonderful additions to a vegetable garden and require nutritious soil and lots of sunlight.

> page 58

Beans are fun to grow. The leaves sprout first, followed by curling tendrils, delicate flowers, and finally, the delicious beans.

> page 59

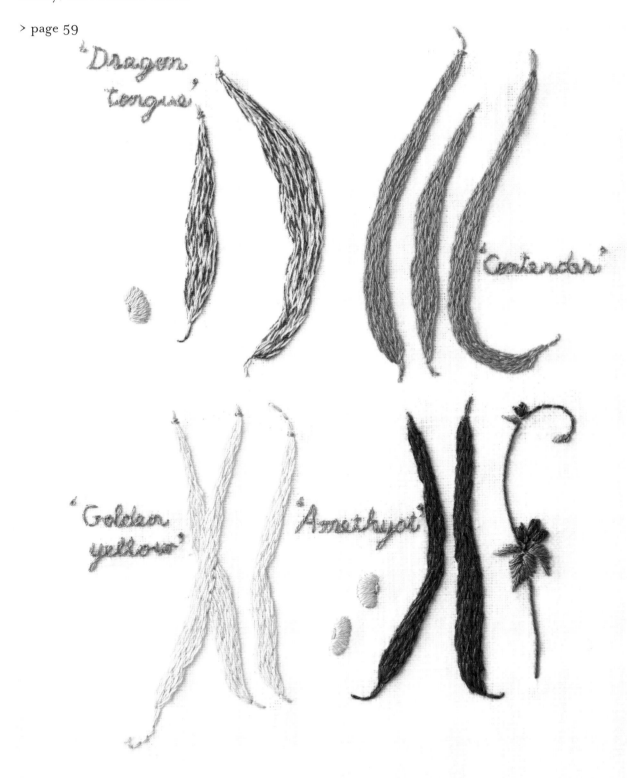

'Dragon tongue'

'Contender'

'Golden yellow'

'Amethyst'

Bean

Known as the 'garden radish,' this variety brings color to your salad. The red to reddish purple tones are very pretty.

> page 60

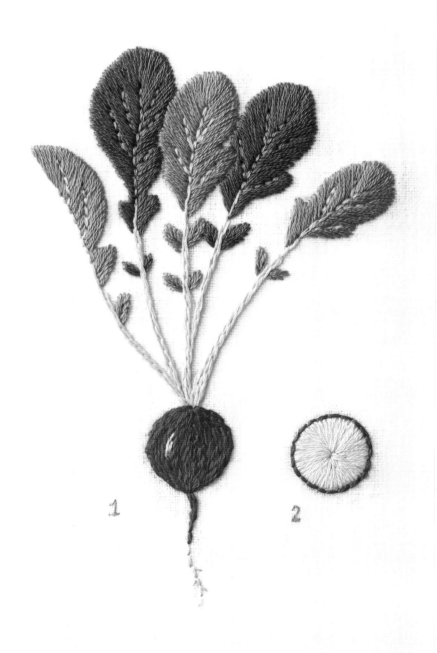

1

2

Radish

Orange may be the classic color of this carotene-rich root vegetable, but yellow and purple varieties are also available, and the inner core of purple carrots is orange.

> page 61

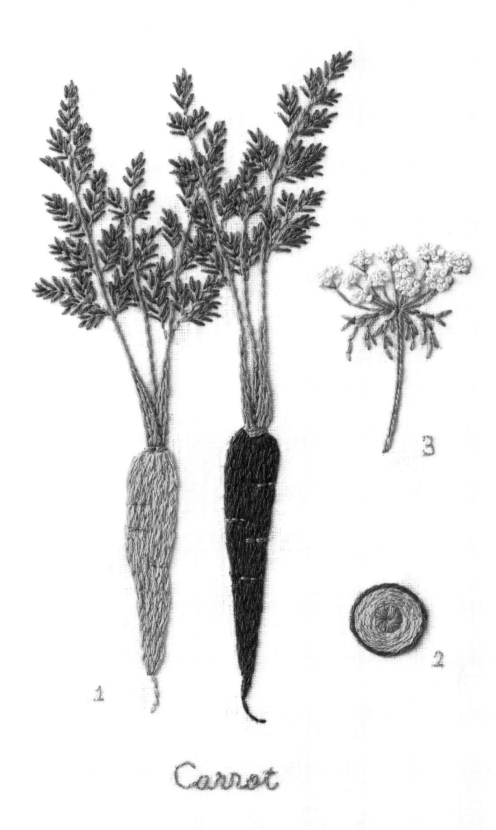

Carrot

Also known as bay leaf, laurel is a useful plant to have in your garden: Besides adding flavor to soups and stews, the leaves also make lovely wreaths.

> page 62

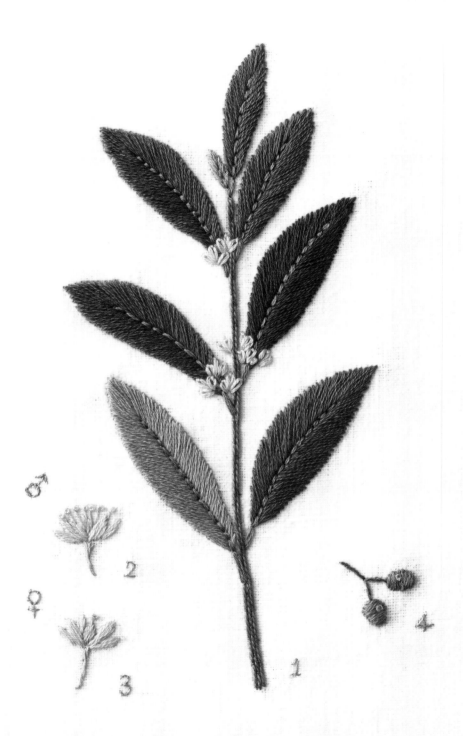

♂
2
♀
3
1
4

Laurel

This herb goes well with fish. In Sweden, boiled potatoes with dill are often eaten in summer.

> page 63

Dill

This plant is often grown in vegetable gardens for color and for use in salads. Both the leaves and flowers have unique colors and shapes that make it a perfect accent.

> page 64

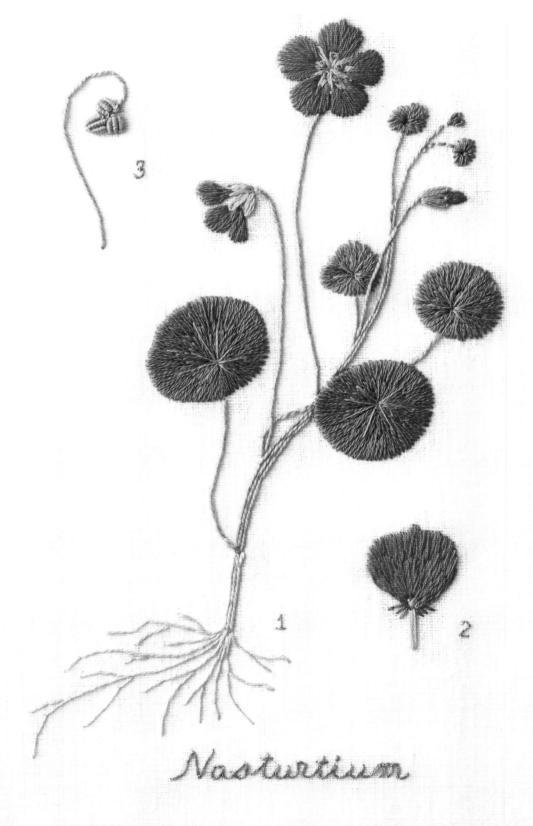

Nasturtium

Rosemary is a must-have herb in your garden, not only for the flavor it adds to your cooking, but also for its gentle savory aroma that wafts up when you simply walk by.

> page 65

1
2

Rosemary

Zucchini is an easy to grow summer squash popular among gardeners. The squash itself is delicious sautéed with olive oil, while fried zucchini blossoms are considered a delicacy.

> page 66

Zucchini

Vegetables often produce simple plain flowers, but okra is in the same family with hibiscus and grows large, gorgeous yellow flowers. They are a colorful addition in a vegetable garden.

> page 67

Okra

This leafy vegetable has a sesame-like fragrance and a spicy flavor. When grown from autumn into winter, the stems will turn red.

> page 68

Rocket

Much to my disappointment, the very first asparagus I grew was about the thickness of a pencil. I realized that in order to grow asparagus as thick as a finger, you need good soil, fertilizer, and plenty of sunlight.

> page 69

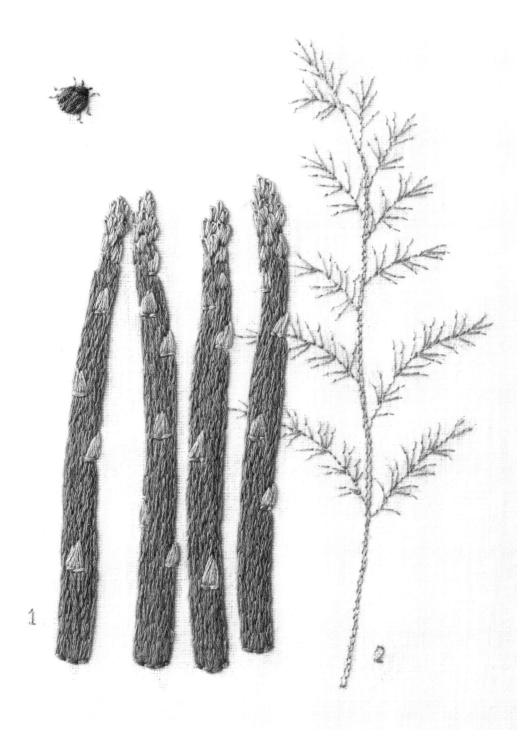

Asparagus

MESCLUN

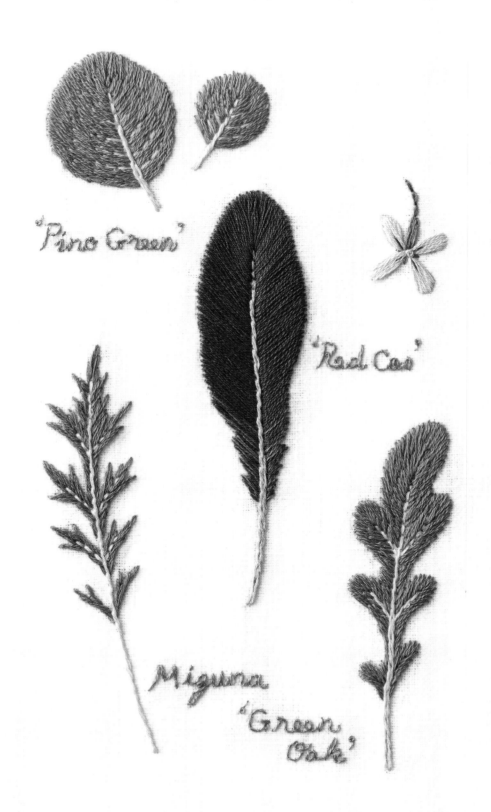

'Pino Green'

'Red Oak'

Mizuna

'Green Oak'

Derived from the French word for mixture, mesclun is an assortment of small, young salad greens known for their combination of colors and flavors. You can even purchase pre-mixed seeds which will yield a variety of greens.

> pages 70-71

Treviso

'Green Curl'

Salvatica

Swiss Chard

'Green Cos'

EDIBLE FLOWER

Dianthus

Viola

Rose

Borage

Nabana

Elegant and colorful, edible flowers are an eye-catching addition to salads or a beautiful way to decorate cakes. Explore growing organic edible flowers as inspiration for recipes, as well as embroidery projects!

> pages 72-73

Primula

Daisy

Narrow-leaved Vetch

Lilac

Cornflower

Nasturtium

MY FAVORITE TOOLS

As with most hobbies, figuring out your favorite tools and materials is a process. Once you have the tools you like best, gardening becomes much more fun. I also love to use my tools as inspiration for embroidery designs.

> pages 74-75

Eggplant is a beautiful vegetable with a deep purple-navy shade. It is hard to embroider because there isn't any single thread color that can match its very unique hue.

> page 76

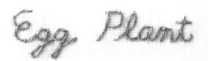

Hot peppers might be pretty, but be careful! Before growing, research different types of chili peppers. Some varieties look like ordinary, mild garden peppers but are extremely hot.

> page 77

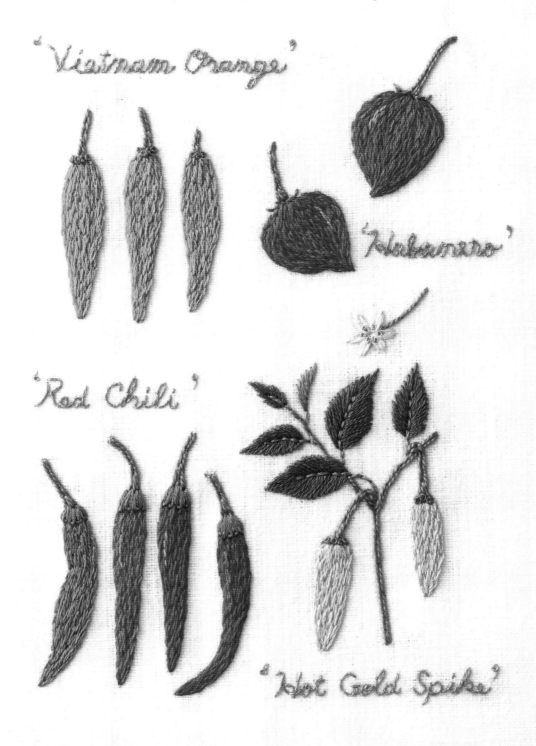

'Vietnam Orange'

'Habanero'

'Red Chili'

'Hot Gold Spike'

Chili Pepper

Have you ever seen Brussels sprouts growing before? These miniature cabbages grow on show-stopping stalks and have large, leafy greens that resemble a palm tree.

> page 78

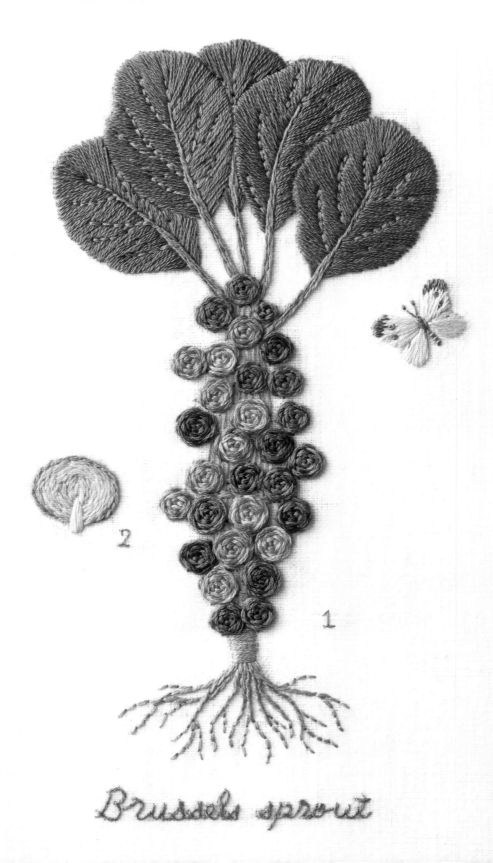

Brussels sprout

Komatsuna is a nutritious green and yellow leaf vegetable. It is high in vitamins A and C and its taste is a cross between mustard and cabbage.

> page 79

Komatsuna

Pumpkin and squash contain an abundance of vitamins and carotene that strengthen the immune system. Their colors are autumnal and inspire a warm harvest palate for meals and embroidery projects.

> pages 80-81

Pumpkin and Squash

'Korinnki'

'Sweet Mamma'

'Butternut'

'Jackpot'

With their dense nutritional value and high yield, potatoes are one of the world's staple crops. The plant produces pretty light purple flowers, while the potatoes themselves grow underground.

> page 82

Potato

Onions are one of the most common pantry vegetables. We eat the bulb, but the plant also produces a stunning round flower composed of dozens of star-shaped blooms.

> page 83

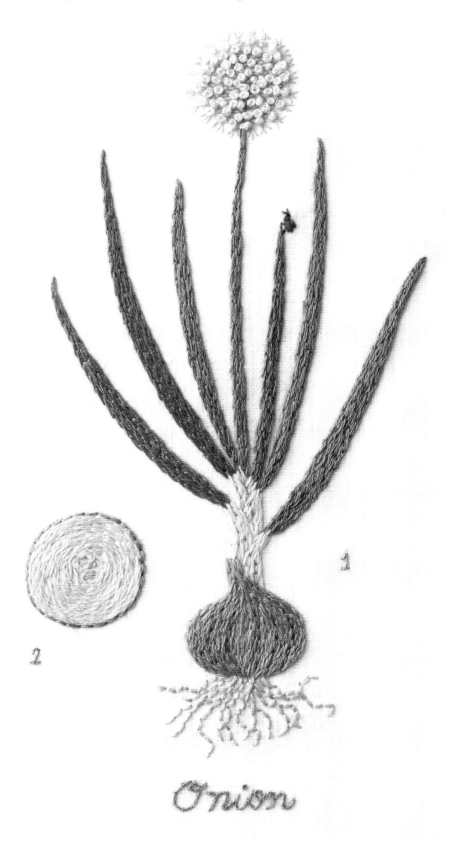

Onion

SPROUT

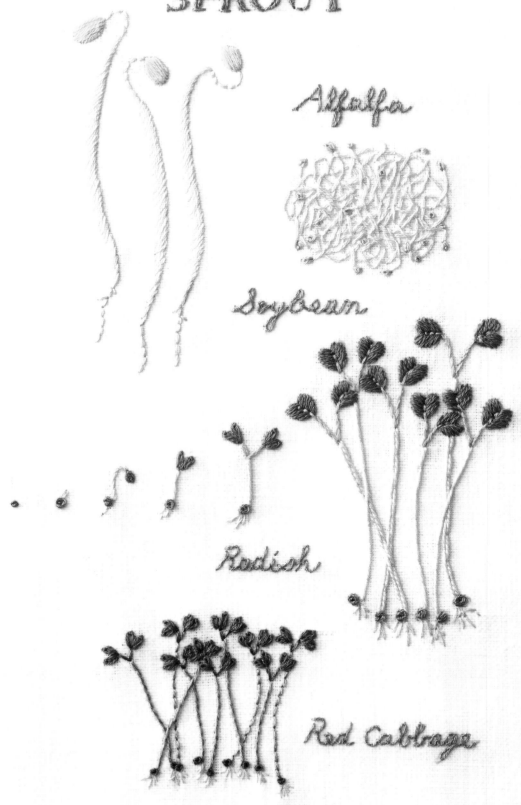

Alfalfa

Soybean

Radish

Red Cabbage

Sprouts are the first growths of plants and often are more nutritious than the fully-matured version of the vegetable. Their spindly little shapes are fun to stitch and are tasty too.

> pages 84-85

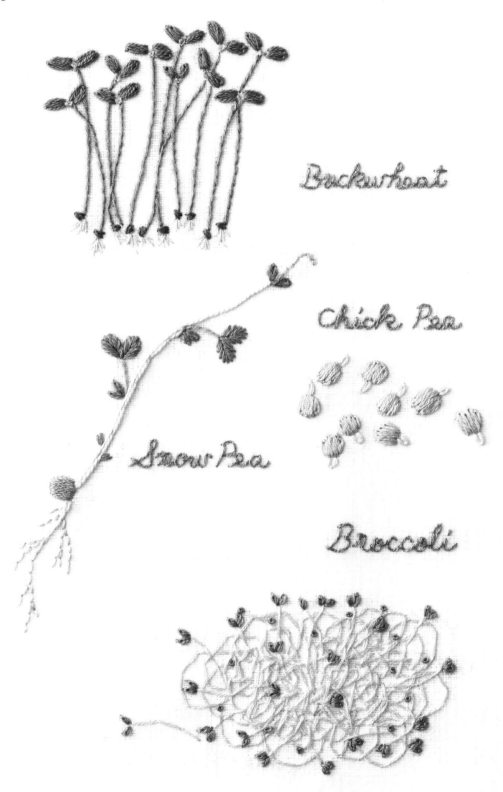

Buckwheat

Chick Pea

Snow Pea

Broccoli

Chives have a more delicate flavor than spring onions. They produce lovely round lilac flowers and are often used to edge the perimeter of kitchen gardens.

> page 86

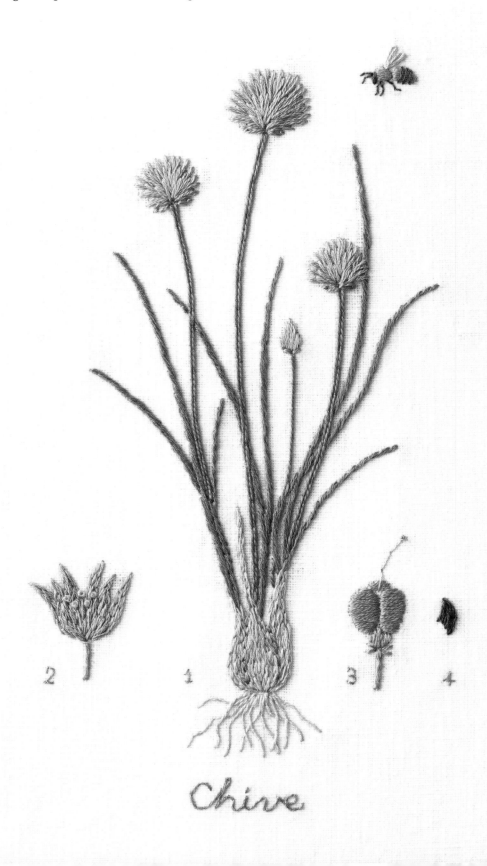

Chive

Marigolds are a time-tested companion plant for vegetable gardens. They ward off unwanted pests and add lovely color to the landscape.

> page 87

Marigold

Not only does parsley add color and aroma to your cooking, it's also a nutritious leafy vegetable. Parsley is known for its propensity to attract butterflies.

> page 88

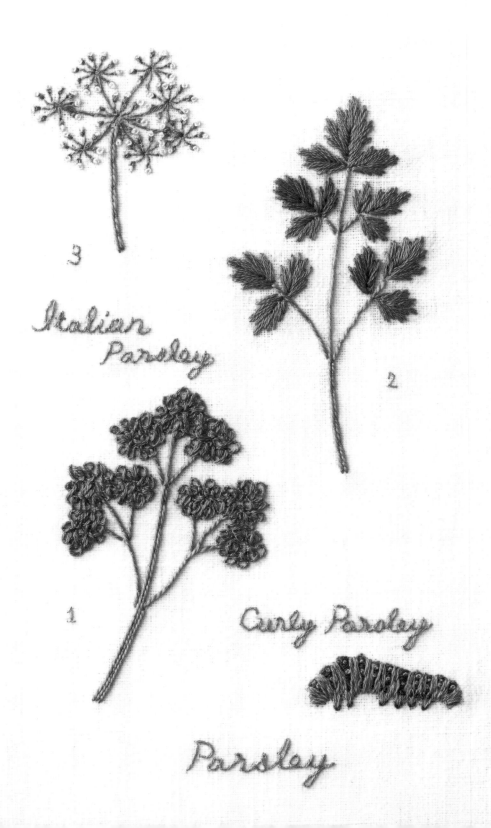

3

Italian Parsley

2

1

Curly Parsley

Parsley

There are many types of sage, but the one we eat is called common sage. It has pretty bluish-purple flowers and is often used in meat dishes.

> page 89

Sage

When your garden gets a little bigger, you'll want to plant fruit trees. The fig tree, with its delicate fruits, also produces fragrant edible leaves.

> page 90

1   2

The juneberry flowers in early spring, its matte red fruits appear in June, and in autumn, you can enjoy its red leaves. It's also a great fruit tree to plant because it is easy to prune.

> page 91

Juneberry

KITCHEN GARDEN VISITORS

A vegetable garden is bound to have an assortment
of visiting creatures! In my garden with fruiting
kumquats, juneberries, and rosehips, first the
birds arrive and then the insects.

> pages 92-93

BEFORE YOU BEGIN

THREAD

DMC No. 25 embroidery floss was used for the majority of designs in this book. This thread is comprised of six easily separated strands, allowing you to adjust the thickness of your stitching by using a different number of strands. To stitch with this thread, cut a 20-24 in (50-60 cm) long piece, separate the strands, then stitch using the designated number of strands. In this book, always use three strands, unless otherwise noted.

Occasionally, you'll be instructed to stitch with more than one color of thread to create depth and shading within your embroidery. In this case, simply combine the designated number of strands of each color, thread the needle, and then stitch as normal.

DMC No. 5 and linen floss are also used to provide contrast and texture. Use one strand of these threads, unless otherwise noted.

Couching stitch is often used in this book to create curved design elements, such as stems and text. With this stitch, the main thread is laid down following the lines of the design, then tacked in place with a separate thread. When working with No. 25 embroidery floss, use the number of strands noted for the main thread and the same or fewer strands for the tacking thread. When working with No. 5 or linen as the main thread, use one strand of No. 25 embroidery floss in a similar color for the tacking thread.

NEEDLES

The relationship between embroidery thread and needles is very important. Choose your needle based on the thickness of your thread and always use sharp needles. Use the following guide to help select the proper needle size:

Thread	Needle
1 strand of No. 5	Size 3-4 embroidery needle
2-3 strands of No. 25	Size 7 embroidery needle
1 strand of No. 25	Thin sewing needle
1 strand of linen	Size 7 embroidery needle

FABRIC

The designs in this book are stitched on 100% linen fabric. For these designs, I like to center the motif on a piece of fabric that is about 12 in (30 cm) wide by 16 in (40 cm) long. If you plan to frame or mount the finished embroidery, you'll want to leave about 4 in (10 cm) of blank fabric around each edge of the design.

I always apply medium-weight fusible interfacing to the wrong side of the fabric before embroidering. The interfacing will prevent the fabric from stretching and helps keep the threads on the back of the work from showing through on the front, giving the piece a more professional finish.

TEMPLATES

All of the templates in this book are full-size. There are several different methods and products you can use to transfer the motifs onto your fabric. I like to trace the motif onto tracing paper. Next, I'll position a sheet of gray carbon chalk paper on the right side of the fabric so that the chalk side faces down. Finally, I'll align the tracing paper on top and use a stylus to trace over the motif. The pressure from the stylus will transfer the chalk from the carbon paper onto the fabric.

HOOPS & FRAMES

Use an embroidery hoop or frame to hold your fabric taut while stitching to create a more professional finish. Use a small hoop for small projects and an adjustable rectangular frame for large projects.

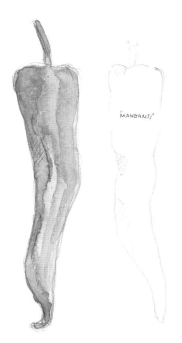

MANGANJI

MY EMBROIDERY TIPS

- I like to use split stitch to fill in vegetables and satin stitch to fill in leaves. Using different stitches for the different elements of the design will add texture and dimension to the work. When using split stitch to fill in round shapes, such as the tomato on page 10 or the eggplant on page 30, start at the midpoint and stitch each half of the outline. Next, fill each half of the shape following the curves of the outline. This will make the stitches appear as if they are radiating from the center and accentuate the round silhouette. When using satin stitch, start from the center of the shape and work toward the shorter ends.

- I like to stitch leaves and flowers from the outside toward the inside. I feel this creates better angles and allows the thread to capture more light.

- You'll get great results if you follow the motifs and stitching instructions, but before you get started, I recommend that you observe actual vegetables or look up photos of vegetables in books or on the Internet. Having a clear image in your mind will help you express yourself more easily when stitching and your needle will not falter.

- Vegetables have their own characteristics that differ from seed to seed and they are raised in different conditions, causing variations in color and shape. No two vegetables are exactly alike—this is part of the beauty of Mother Nature—so don't worry if your embroidery has some slight imperfections.

EMBROIDERY STITCH GUIDE

Note: In this book, the word "stitch" is omitted from the templates in order to save space.

Running Stitch

Use this stitch when you want to add a subtle line or to show movement.

Outline Stitch

A line stitch with volume and texture. When stitched in a line, it can also be used to fill surfaces. Used for stems and roots.

Straight Stitch

The simplest of all embroidery stitches, the straight stitch is mainly used to embroider short lines, such as delicate stems and petals.

Satin Stitch

The glossy appearance and flatness is perfect for petals and leaves. Pull the thread through at a uniform tension to get a clean finish.

Backstitch

This stitch forms a strong line. When stitching curves, keep the stitches short. Used for leaf veins and root tips.

Couching Stitch

This stitch can draw curves freely, so it is ideal for narrow letters, and makes a strong stem when worked in No. 5 floss. Keep the tacking stitches compact for a neat finish.

Split Stitch

Often used to fill in a surface. Not heavy even when used to fill in a large area, like the surface of a leaf. Stitches that are a bit longer will lay flatter.

Padded Satin Stitch

To create a raised effect, make a foundation of several overlapping straight stitches, then cover with satin stitches.

Fly Stitch

Mainly used for calyxes or buds. The tacking stitch can be made a little longer to become a stem.

Leaf Stitch

A convenient stitch that lets you stitch both the leaf and veins at the same time. Make your stitches in a V-shape to produce a classic leaf.

French Knot Stitch (Double Wrapped)

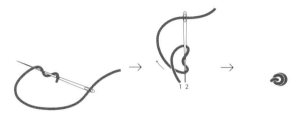

Used for flower pistils, small buds, and seeds. Depending on how tight you pull the thread, the knots can be either hard or soft. In this book, all knots are double wrapped, unless otherwise noted.

Chain Stitch

In this book, this stitch is used as a base for the whipped chain stitch. If you pull the thread taut and make a narrow chain, it can be used as a sturdy line.

Whipped Chain Stitch

After making a line of chain stitch, thread the needle with a different thread and pass the needle under each chain from the same direction. Pass the needle eye first if using a sharp-tipped needle.

Long and Short Stitch

Often used to cover large areas. Be sure to push your needle to the outline of the pattern and insert it into the center.

When stitching the second layer, push the needle out from in between the threads of the first layer, leaving no openings.

Lazy Daisy Stitch

Variations

Used for small flower petals and calyxes.

A straight stitch or satin stitch can be used to fill in the petals. Change the shape by changing the thread tension.

Blanket Stitch

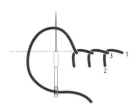

Variation

 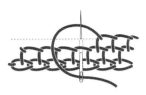

This stitch is often used for appliqué and edging. Choose the spacing and foot length in accordance with the pattern. Also called the buttonhole stitch.

Work one row of chain stitch. Insert your needle through the chain and catch some fabric, then do a blanket stitch. For the next row, stitch halfway in between the blanket stitches of the previous row.

Bullion Stitch A (Bar Type)

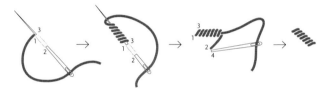

If you wrap the thread around the needle for a bit longer than the length of the fabric you caught, the resulting stitch will be a straight line, and if you wrap it even more, it will become a curve.

Bullion Stitch B (Round Type)

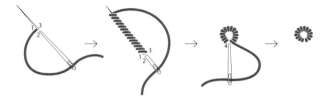

If you only catch a little bit of fabric and wrap the thread around the needle many times, you will get a round shape, and if you wrap it even more, you will get a teardrop shape.

Spider Web Stitch

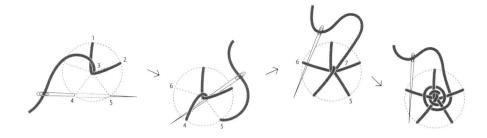

Pass the thread through the center of the circle to create the legs (this example uses five legs), then, starting at the center, weave the thread over and under alternating legs in a spiral pattern.

KITCHEN GARDEN PLANNING

646 (2 strands)
Straight lines: Straight
Long curved lines: Couching
Short curved lines: Outline

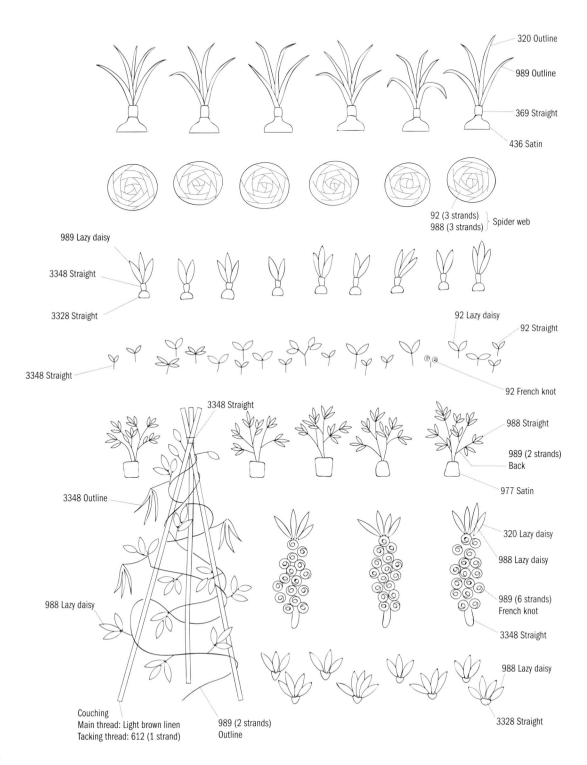

320 Outline

989 Outline

369 Straight

436 Satin

92 (3 strands)
988 (3 strands) } Spider web

989 Lazy daisy

3348 Straight

3328 Straight

92 Lazy daisy

92 Straight

3348 Straight

92 French knot

3348 Straight

988 Straight

989 (2 strands)
Back

3348 Outline

977 Satin

320 Lazy daisy

988 Lazy daisy

989 (6 strands)
French knot

3348 Straight

988 Lazy daisy

988 Lazy daisy

3328 Straight

Couching
Main thread: Light brown linen
Tacking thread: 612 (1 strand)

989 (2 strands)
Outline

KITCHEN GARDEN PLANNING pages 8-9

Materials:
DMC embroidery floss No. 25: 92 (variegated), 153, 168, 320, 365, 369, 436, 612, 645, 646, 729, 822, 841, 977, 988, 989, 3042, 3328, 3348, 3822 / Linen embroidery floss: Brown, light brown

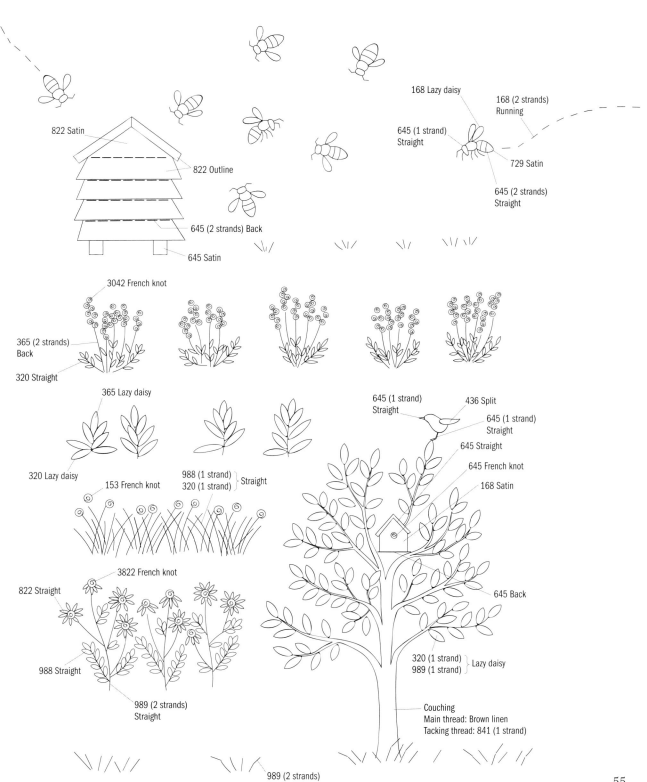

822 Satin

822 Outline

645 (2 strands) Back

645 Satin

168 Lazy daisy

168 (2 strands) Running

645 (1 strand) Straight

729 Satin

645 (2 strands) Straight

3042 French knot

365 (2 strands) Back

320 Straight

365 Lazy daisy

320 Lazy daisy

153 French knot

988 (1 strand)
320 (1 strand) } Straight

645 (1 strand) Straight

436 Split

645 (1 strand) Straight

645 Straight

645 French knot

168 Satin

645 Back

3822 French knot

822 Straight

988 Straight

989 (2 strands) Straight

320 (1 strand)
989 (1 strand) } Lazy daisy

Couching
Main thread: Brown linen
Tacking thread: 841 (1 strand)

989 (2 strands) Straight

Materials:
DMC embroidery floss No. 25: 165, 349, 350, 646, 772, 3023, 3346, 3347, 3822 / No. 5: 3347

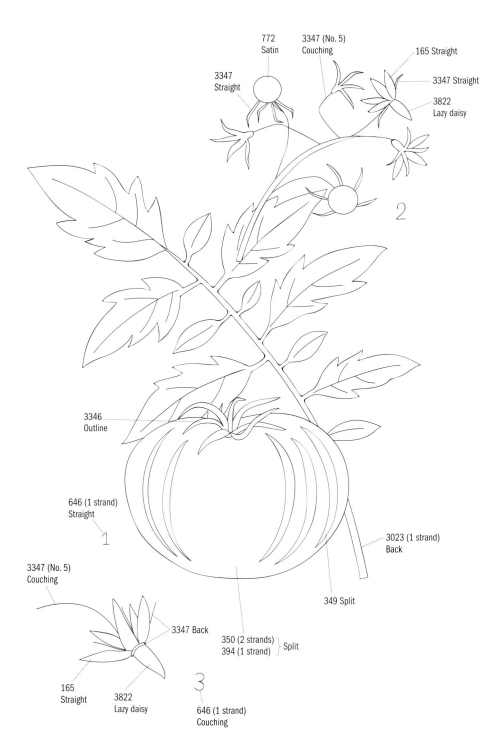

772
Satin

3347 (No. 5)
Couching

165 Straight

3347
Straight

3347 Straight

3822
Lazy daisy

2

3346
Outline

646 (1 strand)
Straight

1

3023 (1 strand)
Back

349 Split

3347 (No. 5)
Couching

3347 Back

350 (2 strands)
394 (1 strand) } Split

165
Straight

3822
Lazy daisy

3

646 (1 strand)
Couching

646 (2 strands) Couching

Tomato

Materials:
DMC embroidery floss No. 25: 152, 165, 347, 349, 350, 352, 470, 646, 728, 3047, 3346, 3347, 3348, 3726, ECRU / No. 5: 3347

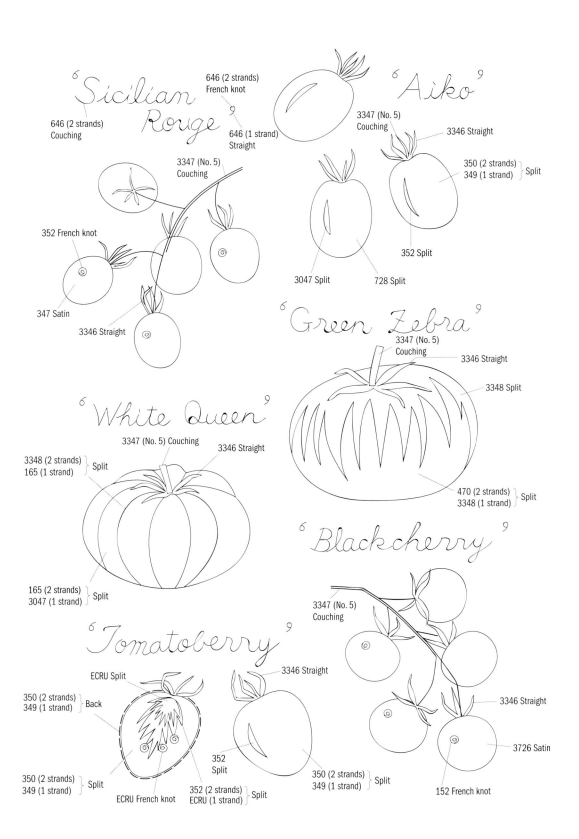

'Sicilian Rouge'

646 (2 strands)
French knot

646 (2 strands)
Couching

646 (1 strand)
Straight

3347 (No. 5)
Couching

352 French knot

347 Satin

3346 Straight

'Aiko'

3347 (No. 5)
Couching

3346 Straight

350 (2 strands) } Split
349 (1 strand)

352 Split

3047 Split

728 Split

'Green Zebra'

3347 (No. 5)
Couching

3346 Straight

3348 Split

470 (2 strands) } Split
3348 (1 strand)

'White Queen'

3347 (No. 5) Couching

3346 Straight

3348 (2 strands) } Split
165 (1 strand)

165 (2 strands) } Split
3047 (1 strand)

'Blackcherry'

3347 (No. 5)
Couching

3346 Straight

3726 Satin

152 French knot

'Tomatoberry'

ECRU Split

350 (2 strands) } Back
349 (1 strand)

3346 Straight

350 (2 strands) } Split
349 (1 strand)

ECRU French knot

352 (2 strands) } Split
ECRU (1 strand)

352
Split

350 (2 strands) } Split
349 (1 strand)

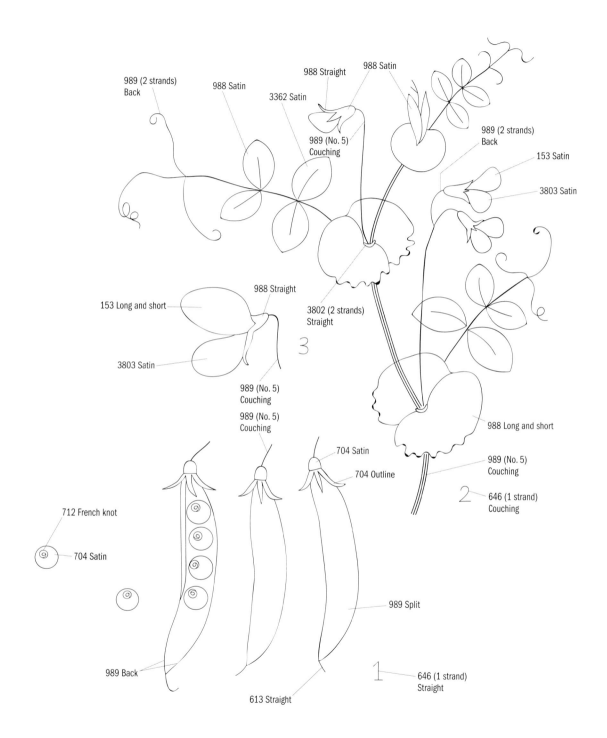

989 (2 strands) Back

988 Satin

3362 Satin

989 (No. 5) Couching

988 Straight

988 Satin

988 Satin

989 (2 strands) Back

153 Satin

3803 Satin

153 Long and short

988 Straight

3803 Satin

3802 (2 strands) Straight

989 (No. 5) Couching

989 (No. 5) Couching

704 Satin

704 Outline

988 Long and short

989 (No. 5) Couching

646 (1 strand) Couching

712 French knot

704 Satin

989 Split

989 Back

646 (1 strand) Straight

613 Straight

646 (2 strand) Couching

Materials:
DMC embroidery floss No. 25: 646, 722, 988, 989, 3021, 3047, 3051, 3348, 3740, 3834, 3863 / No. 5: 3051

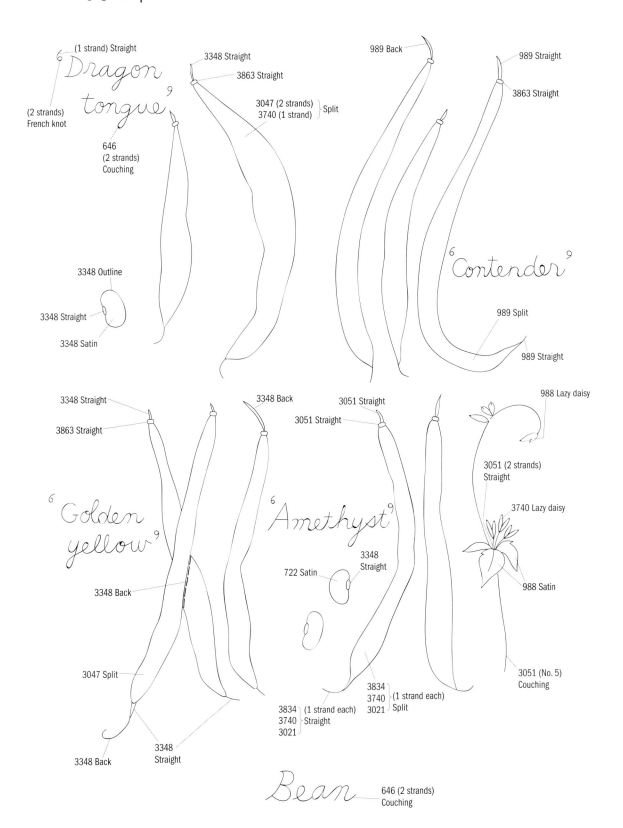

(1 strand) Straight

'Dragon tongue'

(2 strands)
French knot

646
(2 strands)
Couching

3348 Straight

3863 Straight

3047 (2 strands)
3740 (1 strand) } Split

3348 Outline

3348 Straight

3348 Satin

989 Back

989 Straight

3863 Straight

'Contender'

989 Split

989 Straight

3348 Straight

3863 Straight

3348 Back

3051 Straight

3051 Straight

988 Lazy daisy

3051 (2 strands)
Straight

3740 Lazy daisy

'Golden yellow'

'Amethyst'

988 Satin

3348 Back

3047 Split

3348 Back

3348 Straight

722 Satin

3348 Straight

3834
3740 } (1 strand each) Straight
3021

3834
3740 } (1 strand each) Split
3021

3051 (No. 5)
Couching

Bean

646 (2 strands)
Couching

Materials:
DMC embroidery floss No. 25: 304, 347, 646, 772, 989, 3033, 3346, ECRU

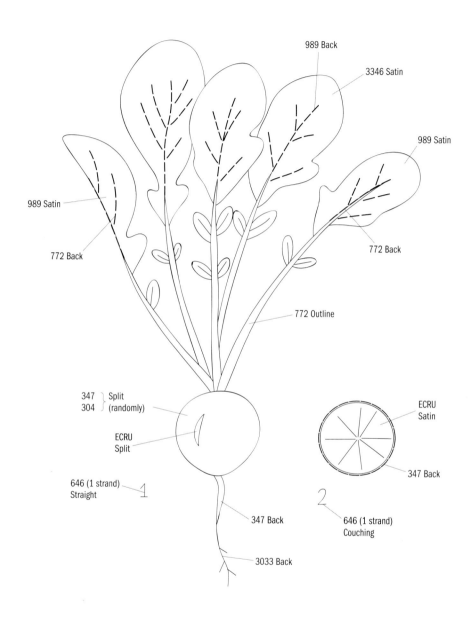

989 Back

3346 Satin

989 Satin

989 Satin

772 Back

772 Back

772 Outline

347 } Split
304 } (randomly)

ECRU
Satin

ECRU
Split

347 Back

646 (1 strand)
Straight

1

2

347 Back

646 (1 strand)
Couching

3033 Back

Radish

646 (2 strands)
Couching

Materials:
DMC embroidery floss No. 25: 646, 779, 976, 977, 989, 3346, 3740, 3790, ECRU / No. 5: 989

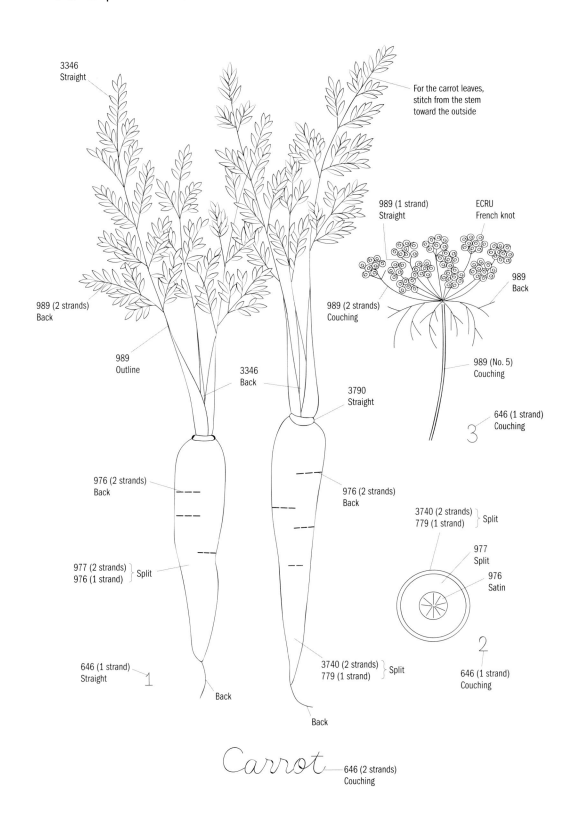

3346
Straight

For the carrot leaves,
stitch from the stem
toward the outside

989 (1 strand)
Straight

ECRU
French knot

989 (2 strands)
Back

989 (2 strands)
Couching

989
Back

989
Outline

3346
Back

989 (No. 5)
Couching

3790
Straight

646 (1 strand)
Couching

976 (2 strands)
Back

976 (2 strands)
Back

3740 (2 strands)
779 (1 strand) } Split

977
Split

976
Satin

977 (2 strands)
976 (1 strand) } Split

646 (1 strand)
Couching

646 (1 strand)
Straight

1

3740 (2 strands)
779 (1 strand) } Split

2

Back

Back

Carrot — 646 (2 strands)
Couching

3

Materials:
DMC embroidery floss No. 25: 165, 368, 646, 987, 3011, 3345, 3347, 3348 / No. 5: 3011

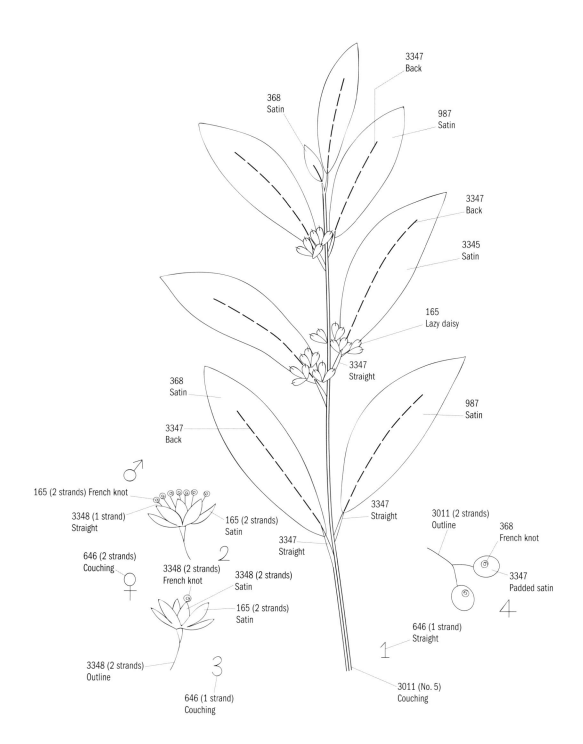

3347
Back

368
Satin

987
Satin

3347
Back

3345
Satin

165
Lazy daisy

3347
Straight

368
Satin

987
Satin

3347
Back

165 (2 strands) French knot

3348 (1 strand)
Straight

165 (2 strands)
Satin

2

646 (2 strands)
Couching

3348 (2 strands)
French knot

3348 (2 strands)
Satin

165 (2 strands)
Satin

3347
Straight

3347
Straight

3011 (2 strands)
Outline

368
French knot

3347
Padded satin

4

3348 (2 strands)
Outline

3

646 (1 strand)
Couching

646 (1 strand)
Straight

1

3011 (No. 5)
Couching

Laurel

646 (2 strands)
Couching

Materials:
DMC embroidery floss No. 25: 470, 646, 727, 729, 822, 844, 989, 3045 3347, 3790 / No. 5: 989

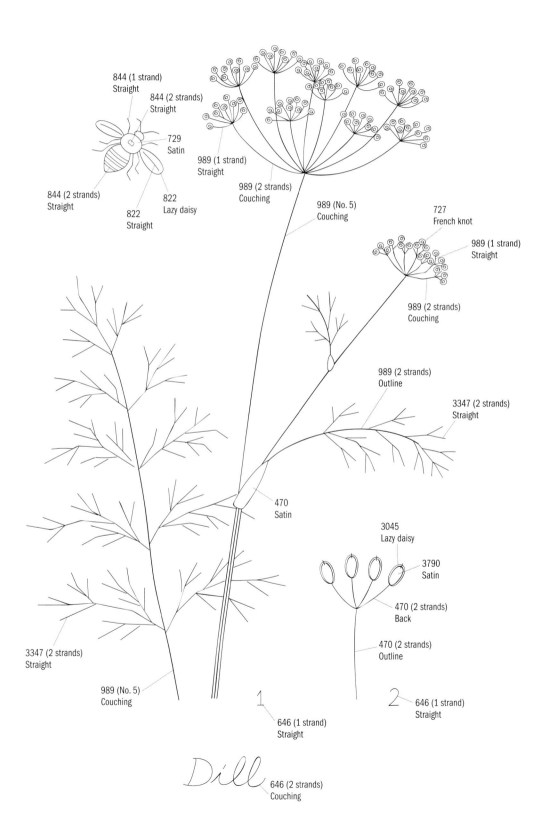

844 (1 strand)
Straight

844 (2 strands)
Straight

729
Satin

844 (2 strands)
Straight

822
Straight

822
Lazy daisy

989 (1 strand)
Straight

989 (2 strands)
Couching

989 (No. 5)
Couching

727
French knot

989 (1 strand)
Straight

989 (2 strands)
Couching

989 (2 strands)
Outline

3347 (2 strands)
Straight

470
Satin

3045
Lazy daisy

3790
Satin

470 (2 strands)
Back

470 (2 strands)
Outline

3347 (2 strands)
Straight

989 (No. 5)
Couching

1

646 (1 strand)
Straight

2

646 (1 strand)
Straight

Dill

646 (2 strands)
Couching

Materials:
DMC embroidery floss No. 25: 613, 646, 720, 783, 988, 989, 3348, 3821 / No. 5: 613, 3348 /
Linen embroidery floss: Tan

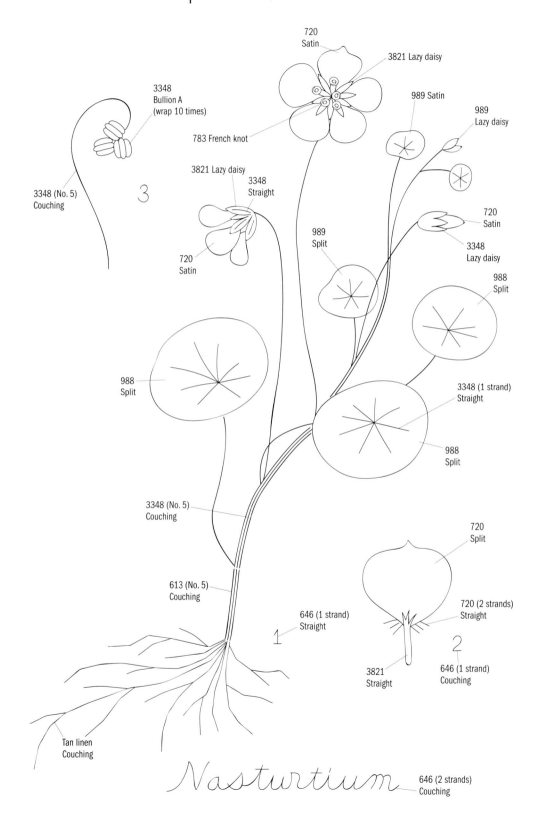

720
Satin

3821 Lazy daisy

989 Satin

989
Lazy daisy

3348
Bullion A
(wrap 10 times)

783 French knot

3348 (No. 5)
Couching

3821 Lazy daisy

3348
Straight

3

720
Satin

989
Split

720
Satin

3348
Lazy daisy

988
Split

988
Split

3348 (1 strand)
Straight

988
Split

3348 (No. 5)
Couching

720
Split

613 (No. 5)
Couching

646 (1 strand)
Straight

720 (2 strands)
Straight

1

2

3821
Straight

646 (1 strand)
Couching

Tan linen
Couching

Nasturtium

646 (2 strands)
Couching

Materials:
DMC embroidery floss No. 25: 159, 160, 317, 646, 772, 989, 3053, 3346 / No. 5: 841, 3053

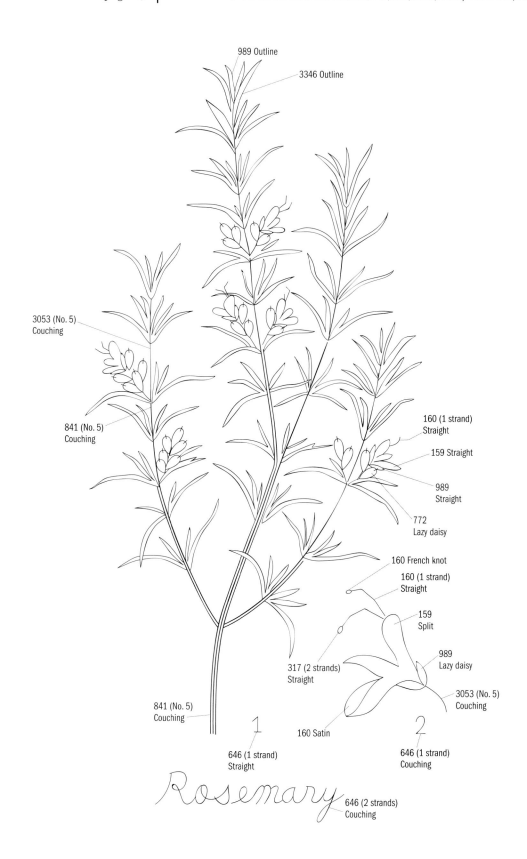

989 Outline

3346 Outline

3053 (No. 5)
Couching

841 (No. 5)
Couching

160 (1 strand)
Straight

159 Straight

989
Straight

772
Lazy daisy

160 French knot

160 (1 strand)
Straight

159
Split

989
Lazy daisy

317 (2 strands)
Straight

3053 (No. 5)
Couching

841 (No. 5)
Couching

1

2

160 Satin

646 (1 strand)
Straight

646 (1 strand)
Couching

Rosemary

646 (2 strands)
Couching

Materials:
DMC embroidery floss No. 25: 165, 646, 987, 988, 989, 3023, 3345, 3821, 3822, 3854

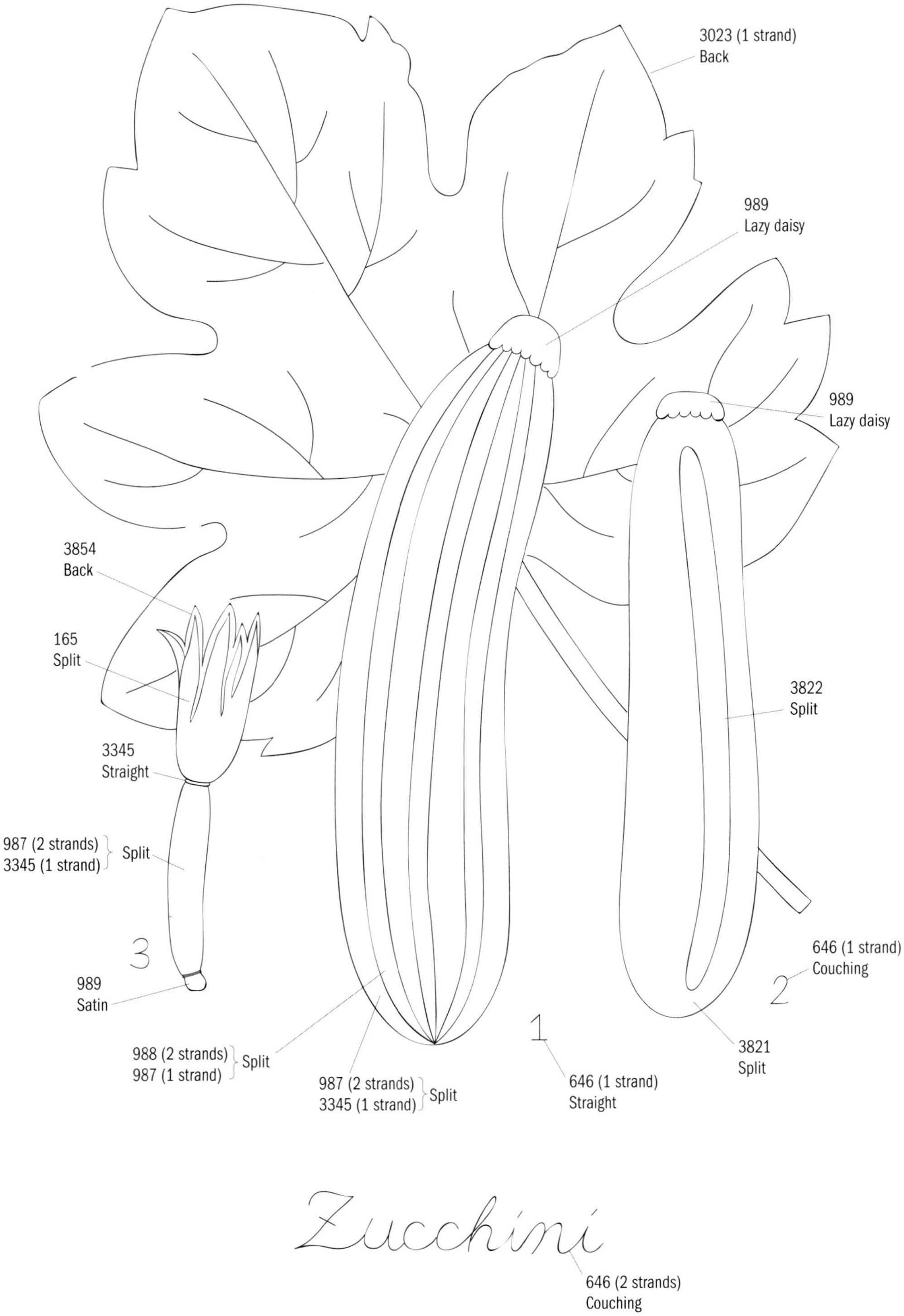

3023 (1 strand)
Back

989
Lazy daisy

989
Lazy daisy

3854
Back

165
Split

3822
Split

3345
Straight

987 (2 strands)
3345 (1 strand) } Split

646 (1 strand)
Couching

989
Satin

988 (2 strands)
987 (1 strand) } Split

987 (2 strands)
3345 (1 strand) } Split

646 (1 strand)
Straight

3821
Split

Zucchini

646 (2 strands)
Couching

Materials:
DMC embroidery floss No. 25: 646, 704, 727, 746, 772, 989, 3023, 3347, 3721, 3803, 3822, 3863 / No. 5: 989 /
Invisible thread / A small piece of tulle or mesh fabric: Moss green

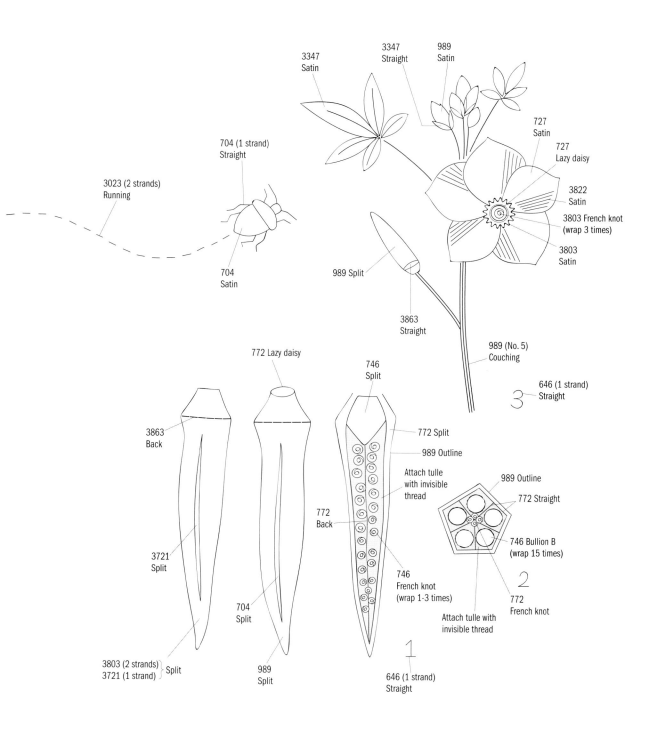

3347
Satin

3347
Straight

989
Satin

727
Satin

727
Lazy daisy

3822
Satin

3803 French knot
(wrap 3 times)

3803
Satin

704 (1 strand)
Straight

3023 (2 strands)
Running

704
Satin

989 Split

3863
Straight

989 (No. 5)
Couching

646 (1 strand)
Straight

3

772 Lazy daisy

746
Split

772 Split

989 Outline

Attach tulle
with invisible
thread

989 Outline

772 Straight

3863
Back

746 Bullion B
(wrap 15 times)

772
Back

3721
Split

772
French knot

2

3803 (2 strands)
3721 (1 strand) } Split

704
Split

746
French knot
(wrap 1-3 times)

989
Split

Attach tulle with
invisible thread

1

646 (1 strand)
Straight

Okra

646 (2 strands)
Couching

Materials:
DMC embroidery floss No. 25: 223, 368, 472, 646, 779, 822, 988, 3051, 3722 / No. 5: 3051, 223

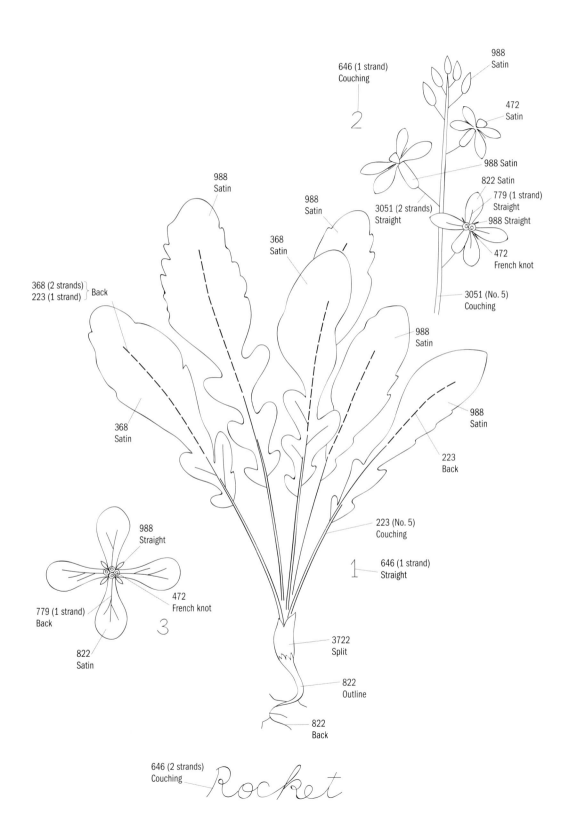

988
Satin

646 (1 strand)
Couching

2

472
Satin

988 Satin

988
Satin

822 Satin

988
Satin

779 (1 strand)
Straight

368
Satin

3051 (2 strands)
Straight

988 Straight

472
French knot

368 (2 strands)
223 (1 strand) } Back

3051 (No. 5)
Couching

988
Satin

368
Satin

988
Satin

223
Back

223 (No. 5)
Couching

988
Straight

1

646 (1 strand)
Straight

472
French knot

779 (1 strand)
Back

3

822
Satin

3722
Split

822
Outline

822
Back

646 (2 strands)
Couching

Rocket

Materials:
DMC embroidery floss No. 25: 647, 841, 844, 989, 3023, 3328, 3347, 3348

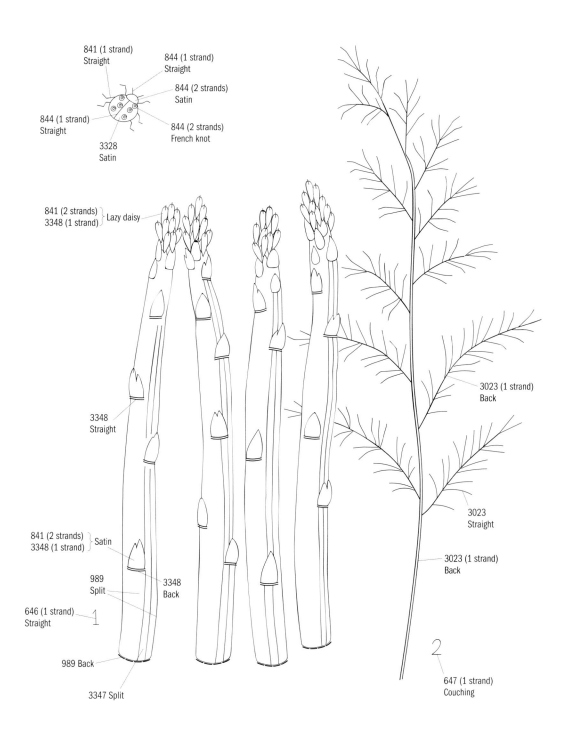

841 (1 strand)
Straight

844 (1 strand)
Straight

844 (2 strands)
Satin

844 (1 strand)
Straight

844 (2 strands)
French knot

3328
Satin

841 (2 strands)
3348 (1 strand) } Lazy daisy

3348
Straight

841 (2 strands)
3348 (1 strand) } Satin

989
Split

3348
Back

646 (1 strand)
Straight

989 Back

3347 Split

3023 (1 strand)
Back

3023
Straight

3023 (1 strand)
Back

647 (1 strand)
Couching

Asparagus

647 (2 strands) Couching

MESCLUN

646 (2 strands)
Straight lines: Straight
Long curved lines: Couching
Short curved lines: Outline

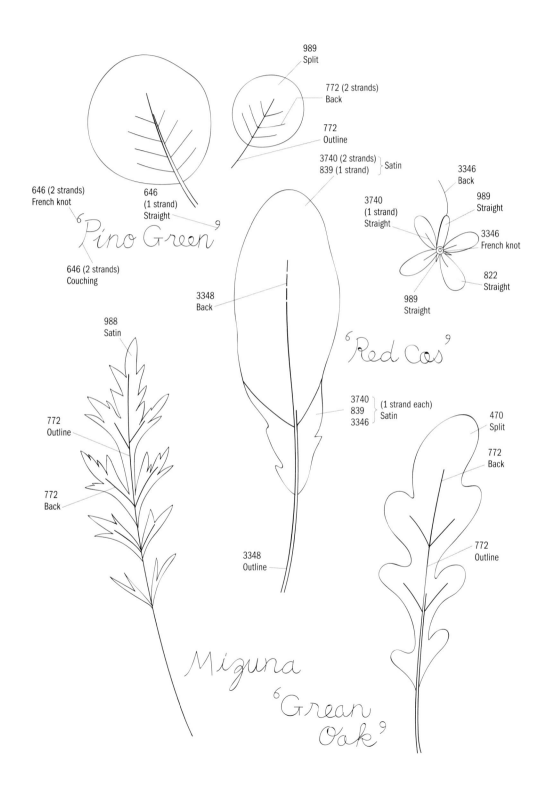

989
Split

772 (2 strands)
Back

772
Outline

3740 (2 strands)
839 (1 strand) } Satin

3346
Back

3740
(1 strand)
Straight

989
Straight

3346
French knot

822
Straight

989
Straight

646 (2 strands)
French knot

646
(1 strand)
Straight

'Pino Green'

646 (2 strands)
Couching

3348
Back

'Red Cos'

988
Satin

772
Outline

772
Back

3740
839   } (1 strand each)
3346 } Satin

470
Split

772
Back

772
Outline

3348
Outline

Mizuna
'Green
Oak'

Materials:
DMC embroidery floss No. 25: 315, 351, 470, 646, 772, 822, 839, 907, 988, 989, 3346, 3348, 3740, 3819

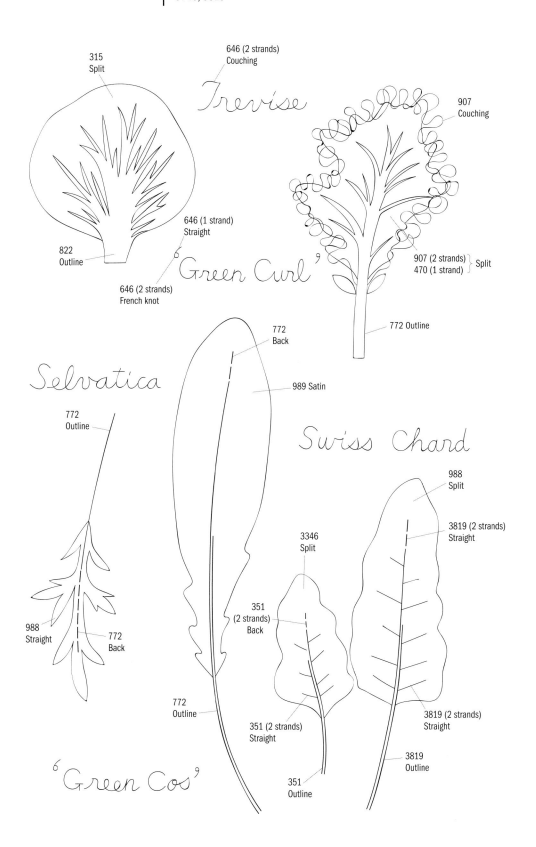

315
Split

646 (2 strands)
Couching

Trevise

907
Couching

822
Outline

646 (1 strand)
Straight

'Green Curl'

907 (2 strands)
470 (1 strand) } Split

646 (2 strands)
French knot

772 Outline

Selvatica

772
Back

989 Satin

772
Outline

Swiss Chard

988
Split

3346
Split

3819 (2 strands)
Straight

988
Straight

772
Back

351
(2 strands)
Back

772
Outline

351 (2 strands)
Straight

3819 (2 strands)
Straight

'Green Cos'

351
Outline

3819
Outline

EDIBLE FLOWER

646 (2 strands)
Straight lines: Straight
Long curved lines: Couching
Short curved lines: Outline

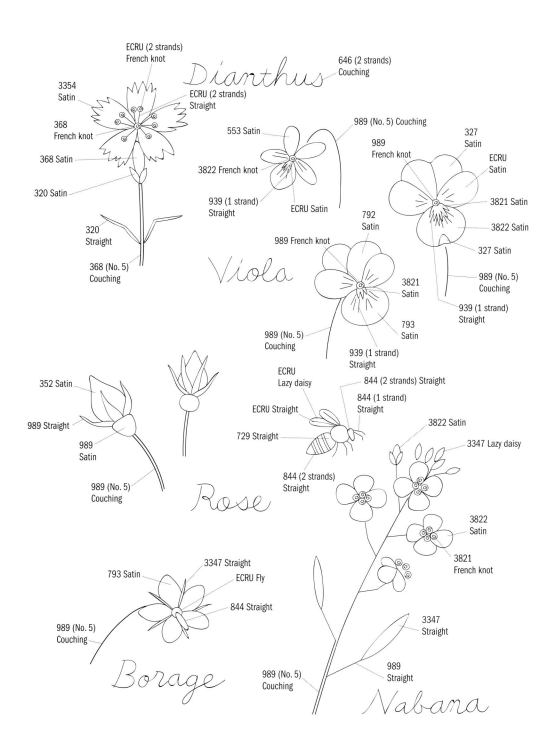

Dianthus

ECRU (2 strands)
French knot

646 (2 strands)
Couching

3354
Satin

ECRU (2 strands)
Straight

368
French knot

368 Satin

320 Satin

320
Straight

368 (No. 5)
Couching

Viola

553 Satin

989 (No. 5) Couching

989
French knot

327
Satin

3822 French knot

ECRU
Satin

939 (1 strand)
Straight

ECRU Satin

3821 Satin

3822 Satin

327 Satin

989 (No. 5)
Couching

939 (1 strand)
Straight

989 French knot

792
Satin

3821
Satin

793
Satin

989 (No. 5)
Couching

939 (1 strand)
Straight

Rose

352 Satin

989 Straight

989
Satin

989 (No. 5)
Couching

ECRU
Lazy daisy

844 (2 strands) Straight

844 (1 strand)
Straight

ECRU Straight

729 Straight

844 (2 strands)
Straight

3822 Satin

3347 Lazy daisy

3822
Satin

3821
French knot

3347 Straight

793 Satin

ECRU Fly

844 Straight

989 (No. 5)
Couching

Borage

3347
Straight

989
Straight

989 (No. 5)
Couching

Nabana

EDIBLE FLOWERS

pages 26-27

Materials:
DMC embroidery floss No. 25: 320, 327, 352, 368, 553, 554, 646, 729, 792, 793, 840, 844, 922, 939, 989, 3347, 3348, 3354, 3607, 3608, 3821, 3822, ECRU / No. 5: 368, 989, 3348

Primula

646 (2 strands)
Couching

3822 Satin

3821
Straight

989
Lazy daisy

989 (No. 5)
Couching

989
French knot

Daisy

ECRU
Lazy daisy

989 (2 strands)
Back

3354 Satin

3821
French knot

3354
Straight

3347
Lazy daisy

989 (No. 5)
Couching

Narrow-leaved Vetch

989 Back

3347
Lazy daisy

989
(2 strands) Back

3608 Satin

3607
Lazy daisy

989
Straight

989 (No. 5)
Couching

Lilac

545
Straight

554 French knot

554
Straight

989 (2 strands)
French knot

989
Straight

554
Lazy daisy

554
Straight

989 (No. 5)
Couching

793
Satin

368 Satin

840
(2 strands)
Fly

368 (No. 5)
Couching

Coanflower

Nasturtium

922
Satin

3821
Lazy daisy

3821
Straight

729
French knot

3348 (No. 5)
Couching

3348
Lazy daisy

922 Satin

73

MY FAVORITE TOOLS

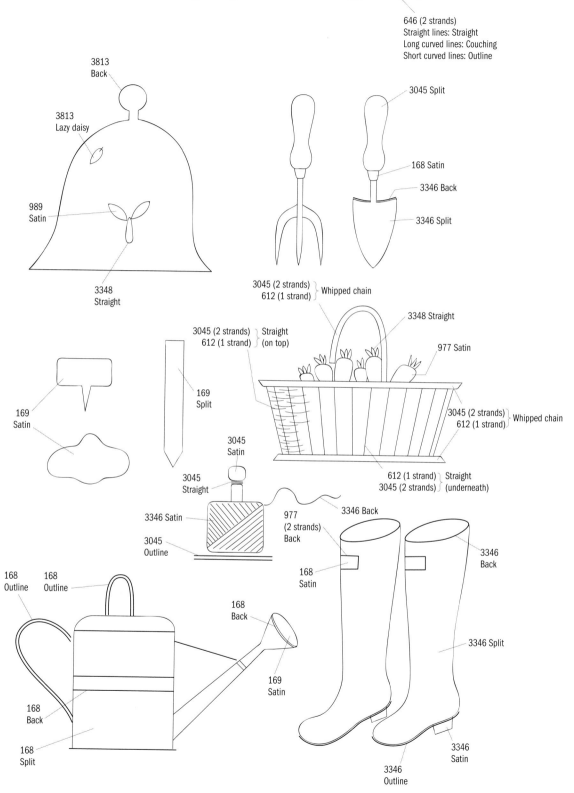

646 (2 strands)
Straight lines: Straight
Long curved lines: Couching
Short curved lines: Outline

3813
Back

3813
Lazy daisy

3045 Split

989
Satin

168 Satin

3346 Back

3346 Split

3348
Straight

3045 (2 strands)
612 (1 strand) } Whipped chain

3348 Straight

977 Satin

3045 (2 strands)
612 (1 strand) } Straight (on top)

169
Satin

169
Split

3045 (2 strands)
612 (1 strand) } Whipped chain

3045
Satin

3045
Straight

3346 Satin

3045
Outline

977
(2 strands)
Back

3346 Back

168
Satin

3346
Back

612 (1 strand)
3045 (2 strands) } Straight (underneath)

168
Outline

168
Outline

168
Back

3346 Split

168
Back

169
Satin

168
Split

3346
Outline

3346
Satin

MY FAVORITE TOOLS
pages 28-29

Materials:
DMC embroidery floss No. 25: 168,169,435, 436, 612, 646, 977, 989, 3045, 3346, 3348, 3813 /
Linen embroidery floss: Brown, light brown

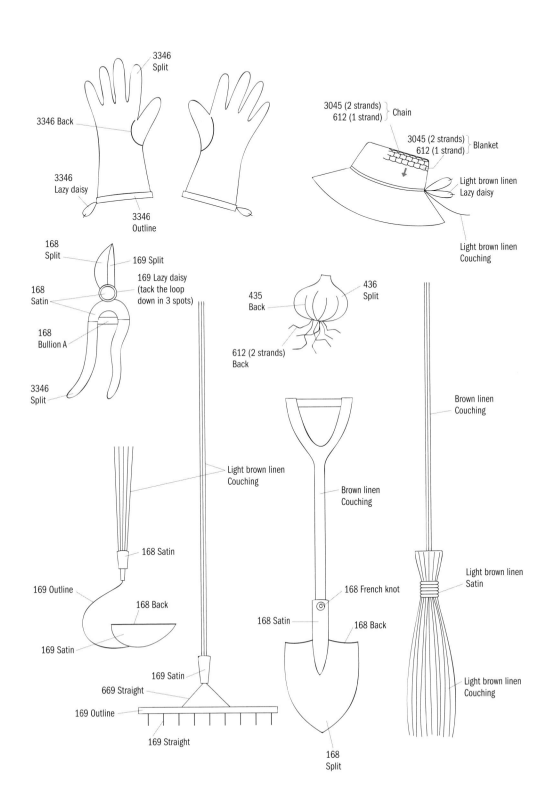

3346
Split

3346 Back

3346
Lazy daisy

3346
Outline

3045 (2 strands) } Chain
612 (1 strand) }

3045 (2 strands) } Blanket
612 (1 strand) }

Light brown linen
Lazy daisy

Light brown linen
Couching

168
Split

169 Split

169 Lazy daisy
(tack the loop
down in 3 spots)

168
Satin

168
Bullion A

3346
Split

435
Back

436
Split

612 (2 strands)
Back

Brown linen
Couching

Light brown linen
Couching

168 Satin

169 Outline

168 Back

169 Satin

169 Satin

669 Straight

169 Outline

169 Straight

Brown linen
Couching

168 French knot

168 Satin

168 Back

168
Split

Light brown linen
Satin

Light brown linen
Couching

Materials:
DMC embroidery floss No. 25: 154, 209, 327, 646, 3023, 3347, 3348, 3371, 3821, ECRU

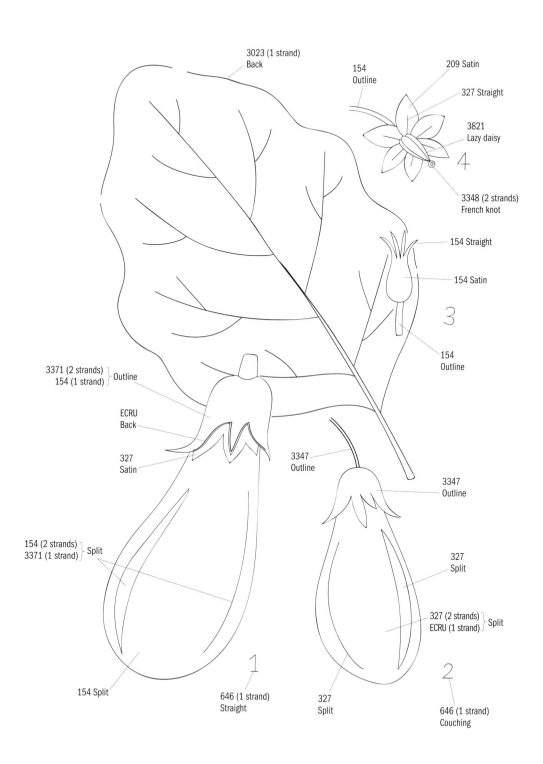

3023 (1 strand)
Back

154
Outline

209 Satin

327 Straight

3821
Lazy daisy

3348 (2 strands)
French knot

4

154 Straight

154 Satin

3

154
Outline

3371 (2 strands)
154 (1 strand) } Outline

ECRU
Back

327
Satin

3347
Outline

3347
Outline

327
Split

327 (2 strands)
ECRU (1 strand) } Split

154 (2 strands)
3371 (1 strand) } Split

154 Split

1

646 (1 strand)
Straight

327
Split

2

646 (1 strand)
Couching

Egg Plant

646 (2 strands)
Couching

Materials:
DMC embroidery floss No. 25: 347, 349, 350, 472, 646, 729, 988, 3346, 3853, ECRU / No. 5: 988

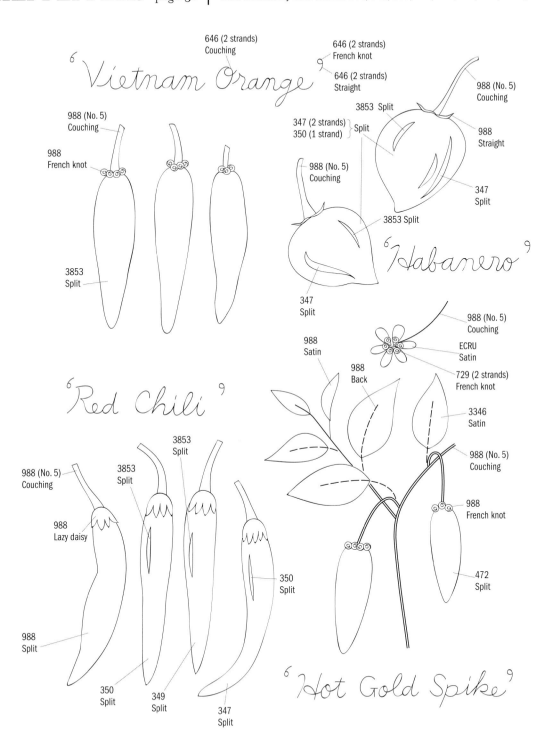

'Vietnam Orange'

646 (2 strands)
Couching

988 (No. 5)
Couching

988
French knot

3853
Split

646 (2 strands)
French knot

646 (2 strands)
Straight

3853 Split

347 (2 strands)
350 (1 strand) } Split

988 (No. 5)
Couching

3853 Split

347
Split

988 (No. 5)
Couching

988
Straight

347
Split

'Habanero'

'Red Chili'

988 (No. 5)
Couching

988
Lazy daisy

988
Split

3853
Split

3853
Split

350
Split

350
Split

349
Split

347
Split

988
Satin

988
Back

988 (No. 5)
Couching

ECRU
Satin

729 (2 strands)
French knot

3346
Satin

988 (No. 5)
Couching

988
French knot

472
Split

'Hot Gold Spike'

Chili Pepper

646 (2 strands)
Couching

Materials:
DMC embroidery floss No. 25: 92 (variegated), 320, 368, 646, 988, 3363, 3782, ECRU

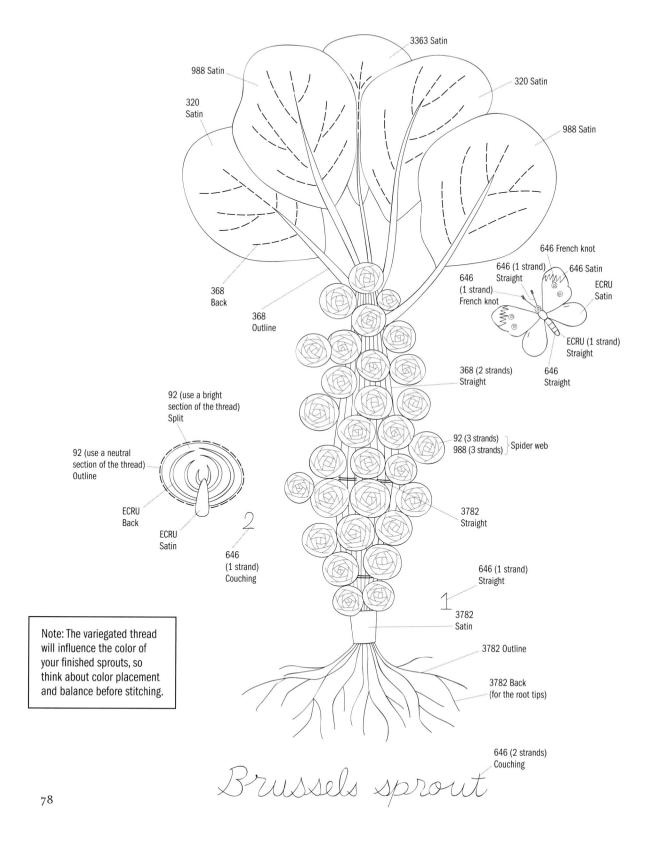

3363 Satin

988 Satin

320 Satin

320
Satin

988 Satin

646 French knot

646 (1 strand)
Straight

646 Satin

646
(1 strand)
French knot

ECRU
Satin

ECRU (1 strand)
Straight

368
Back

368
Outline

368 (2 strands)
Straight

646
Straight

92 (use a bright
section of the thread)
Split

92 (3 strands)
988 (3 strands) } Spider web

92 (use a neutral
section of the thread)
Outline

3782
Straight

ECRU
Back

ECRU
Satin

646
(1 strand)
Couching

646 (1 strand)
Straight

3782
Satin

3782 Outline

3782 Back
(for the root tips)

Note: The variegated thread
will influence the color of
your finished sprouts, so
think about color placement
and balance before stitching.

646 (2 strands)
Couching

Brussels sprout

Materials:
DMC embroidery floss No. 25: 164, 646, 729, 772, 822, 988, 989, 3363, 3822

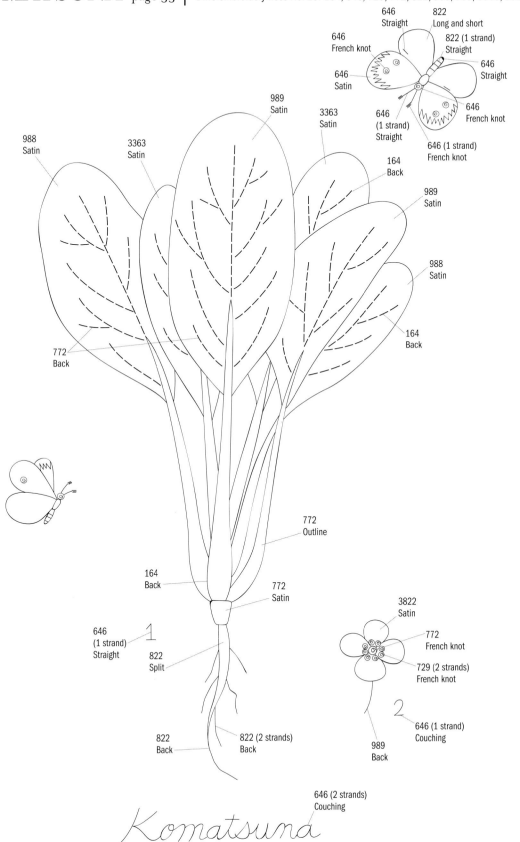

646
Straight

822
Long and short

646
French knot

822 (1 strand)
Straight

646
Straight

646
Satin

646
French knot

646
(1 strand)
Straight

646 (1 strand)
French knot

989
Satin

3363
Satin

164
Back

989
Satin

988
Satin

3363
Satin

988
Satin

164
Back

772
Back

772
Outline

164
Back

772
Satin

646
(1 strand)
Straight

822
Split

3822
Satin

772
French knot

729 (2 strands)
French knot

646 (1 strand)
Couching

989
Back

822
Back

822 (2 strands)
Back

646 (2 strands)
Couching

Komatsuna

Materials:
DMC embroidery floss No. 25: 613, 646, 704, 729, 746, 783, 976, 989, 3045, 3053, 3345, 3346, 3347, 3362, 3820, 3822 / No. 5: 989

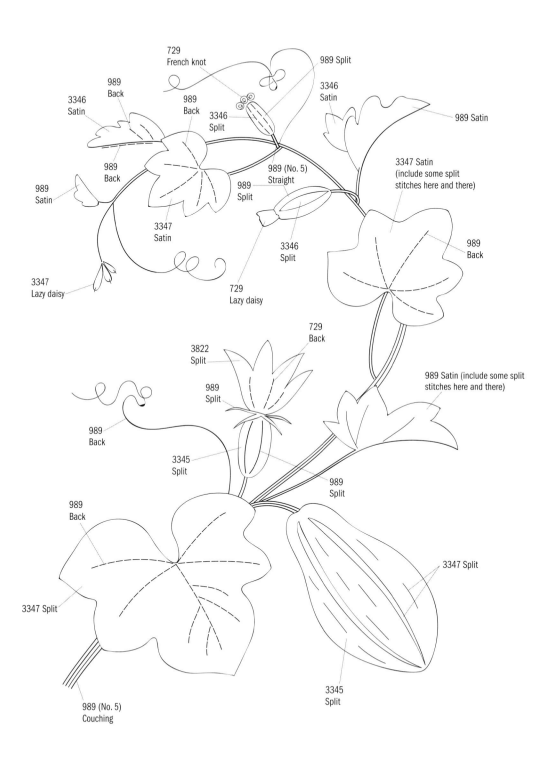

729
French knot

989 Split

989
Back

3346
Satin

3346
Satin

989 Satin

989
Back

3346
Split

989
Back

3347 Satin
(include some split
stitches here and there)

989
Satin

989 (No. 5)
Straight

989
Split

989
Back

3347
Satin

3346
Split

3347
Lazy daisy

729
Lazy daisy

729
Back

3822
Split

989
Split

989 Satin (include some split
stitches here and there)

989
Back

3345
Split

989
Split

989
Back

3347 Split

3347 Split

3345
Split

989 (No. 5)
Couching

646 (2 strands)
Couching

Pumpkin and Squash

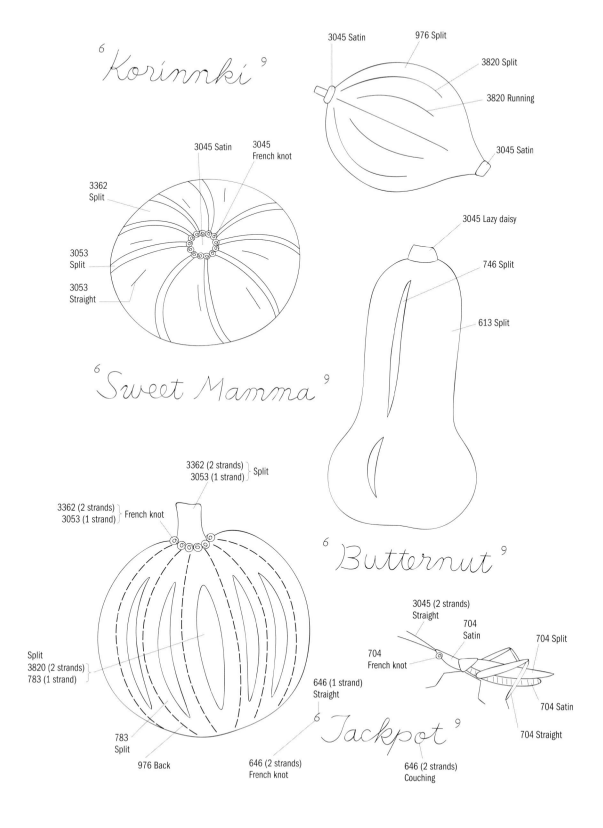

'Korinnki'

3045 Satin

976 Split

3820 Split

3820 Running

3045 Satin

3045 Satin

3045 French knot

3362 Split

3053 Split

3053 Straight

'Sweet Mamma'

3045 Lazy daisy

746 Split

613 Split

'Butternut'

3362 (2 strands)
3053 (1 strand) } Split

3362 (2 strands)
3053 (1 strand) } French knot

Split
3820 (2 strands)
783 (1 strand) }

783 Split

976 Back

646 (1 strand) Straight

646 (2 strands) French knot

'Jackpot'

3045 (2 strands) Straight

704 Satin

704 French knot

704 Split

704 Satin

704 Straight

646 (2 strands) Couching

Materials:
DMC embroidery floss No. 25: 167, 211, 422, 612, 646, 772, 989, 3347, 3363, 3820, No. 5: 612, 3347

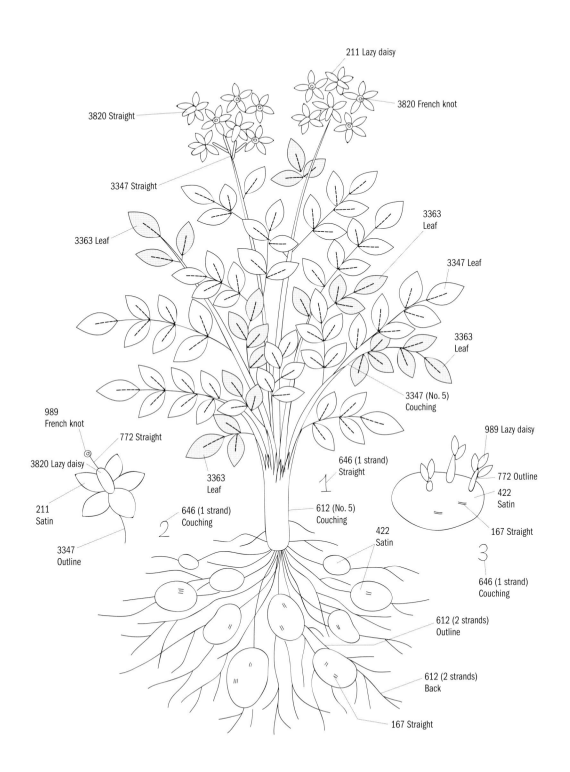

211 Lazy daisy

3820 French knot

3820 Straight

3347 Straight

3363 Leaf

3363 Leaf

3347 Leaf

3363 Leaf

3347 (No. 5) Couching

989 French knot

772 Straight

3820 Lazy daisy

211 Satin

3347 Outline

989 Lazy daisy

772 Outline

422 Satin

167 Straight

3363 Leaf

646 (1 strand) Straight

646 (1 strand) Couching

612 (No. 5) Couching

422 Satin

646 (1 strand) Couching

612 (2 strands) Outline

612 (2 strands) Back

167 Straight

646 (2 strands) Couching

ONION page 37

Materials:
DMC embroidery floss No. 25: 163, 320, 347, 369, 435, 436, 613, 646, 844, ECRU /
A small piece of tulle or mesh fabric: Green

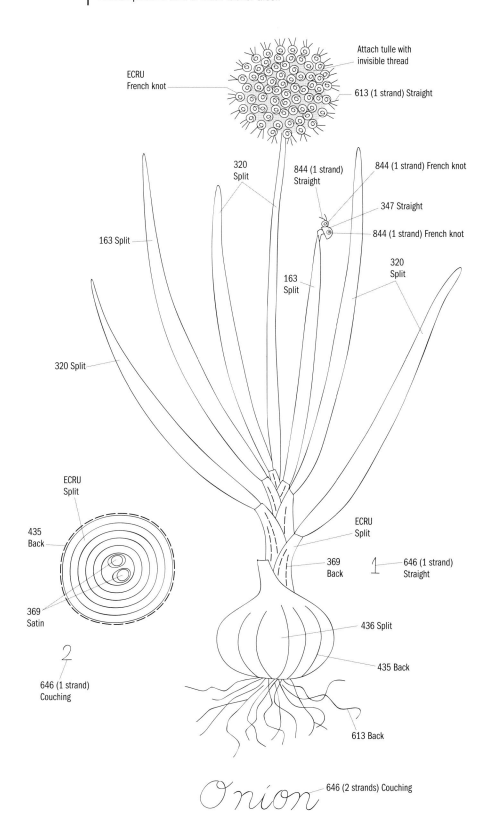

Attach tulle with
invisible thread

ECRU
French knot

613 (1 strand) Straight

320
Split

844 (1 strand)
Straight

844 (1 strand) French knot

347 Straight

844 (1 strand) French knot

163 Split

163
Split

320
Split

320 Split

ECRU
Split

ECRU
Split

435
Back

369
Back

646 (1 strand)
Straight

369
Satin

436 Split

435 Back

2

646 (1 strand)
Couching

613 Back

Onion — 646 (2 strands) Couching

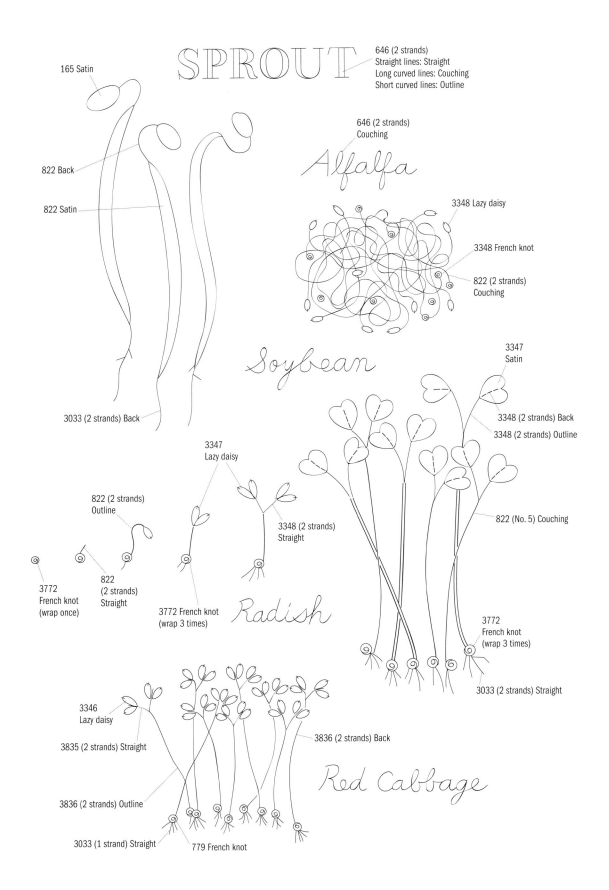

SPROUT

646 (2 strands)
Straight lines: Straight
Long curved lines: Couching
Short curved lines: Outline

165 Satin

822 Back

822 Satin

3033 (2 strands) Back

646 (2 strands)
Couching

Alfalfa

3348 Lazy daisy

3348 French knot

822 (2 strands)
Couching

Soybean

3347
Satin

3348 (2 strands) Back

3348 (2 strands) Outline

822 (No. 5) Couching

3772
French knot
(wrap 3 times)

3033 (2 strands) Straight

3347
Lazy daisy

3348 (2 strands)
Straight

3772 French knot
(wrap 3 times)

Radish

822 (2 strands)
Outline

3772
French knot
(wrap once)

822
(2 strands)
Straight

3346
Lazy daisy

3835 (2 strands) Straight

3836 (2 strands) Back

3836 (2 strands) Outline

Red Cabbage

3033 (1 strand) Straight

779 French knot

Materials:
DMC embroidery floss No. 25: 165, 612, 645, 646, 738, 779, 822, 989, 3033, 3346, 3347, 3348, 3712, 3772, 3835, 3836 / No. 5: 822

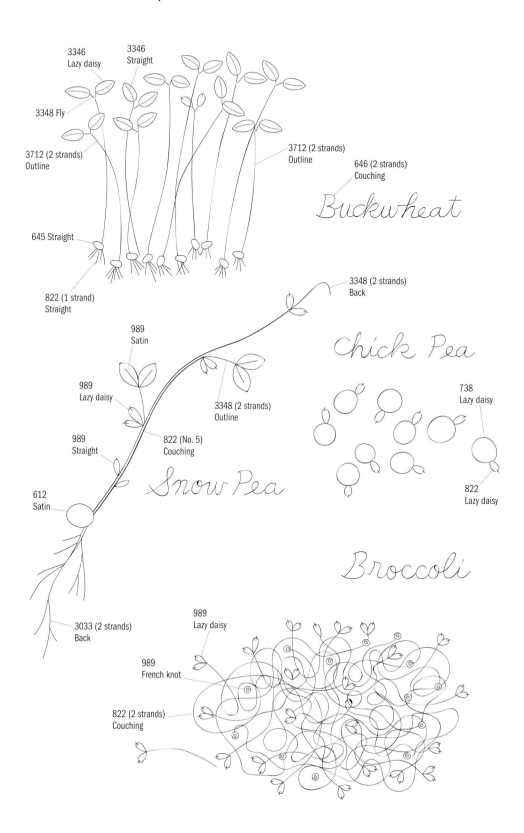

3346
Lazy daisy

3346
Straight

3348 Fly

3712 (2 strands)
Outline

3712 (2 strands)
Outline

646 (2 strands)
Couching

Buckwheat

645 Straight

822 (1 strand)
Straight

3348 (2 strands)
Back

989
Satin

Chick Pea

989
Lazy daisy

3348 (2 strands)
Outline

989
Straight

822 (No. 5)
Couching

738
Lazy daisy

612
Satin

Snow Pea

822
Lazy daisy

Broccoli

3033 (2 strands)
Back

989
Lazy daisy

989
French knot

822 (2 strands)
Couching

CHIVES page 40

Materials:
DMC embroidery floss No. 25: 168, 554, 613, 646, 729, 844, 988, 3045, 3364, 3608 / No. 5: 988 /
Linen embroidery floss: Tan

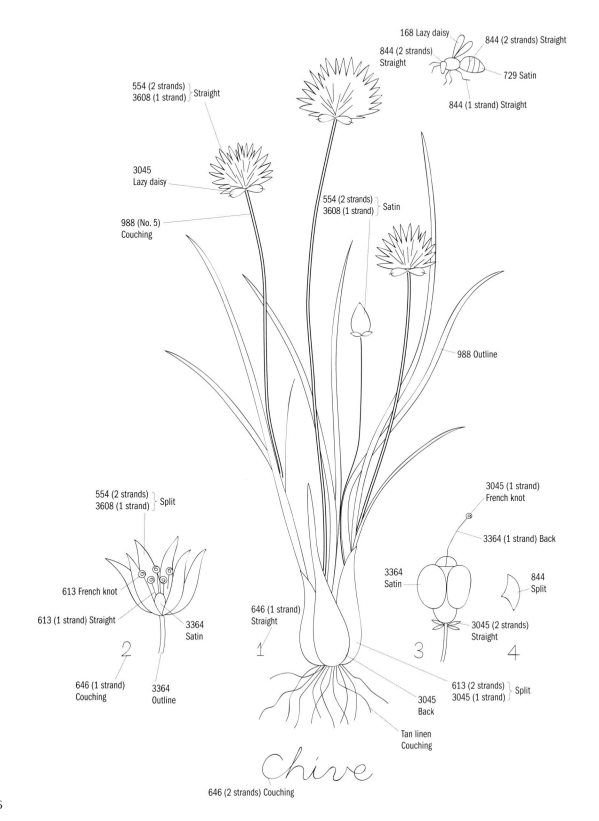

168 Lazy daisy

844 (2 strands)
Straight

844 (2 strands) Straight

729 Satin

844 (1 strand) Straight

554 (2 strands)
3608 (1 strand) } Straight

3045
Lazy daisy

988 (No. 5)
Couching

554 (2 strands)
3608 (1 strand) } Satin

988 Outline

554 (2 strands)
3608 (1 strand) } Split

3045 (1 strand)
French knot

3364 (1 strand) Back

613 French knot

844
Split

613 (1 strand) Straight

3364
Satin

3364
Satin

646 (1 strand)
Straight

3045 (2 strands)
Straight

2

1

3

4

646 (1 strand)
Couching

3364
Outline

613 (2 strands)
3045 (1 strand) } Split

3045
Back

Tan linen
Couching

Chive

646 (2 strands) Couching

MARIGOLD page 41

Materials:
DMC embroidery floss No. 25: 168, 613, 646, 742, 844, 989, 3347, 3348, 3363, 3863 / No. 5: 989 /
Linen embroidery floss: Tan

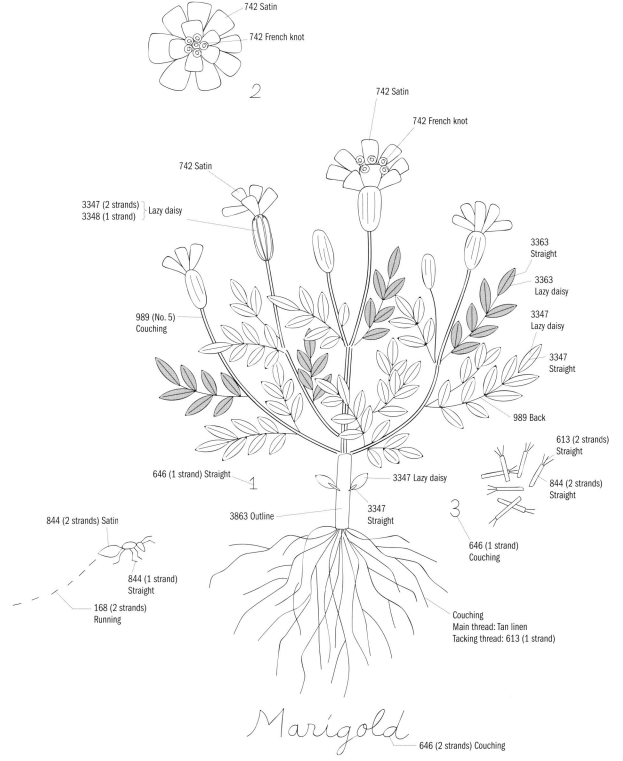

742 Satin

742 French knot

2

742 Satin

742 French knot

742 Satin

3347 (2 strands) } Lazy daisy
3348 (1 strand)

3363
Straight

3363
Lazy daisy

3347
Lazy daisy

3347
Straight

989 (No. 5)
Couching

989 Back

613 (2 strands)
Straight

844 (2 strands)
Straight

646 (1 strand) Straight   1   3347 Lazy daisy

3

3863 Outline   3347
Straight

646 (1 strand)
Couching

844 (2 strands) Satin

844 (1 strand)
Straight

168 (2 strands)
Running

Couching
Main thread: Tan linen
Tacking thread: 613 (1 strand)

Marigold

646 (2 strands) Couching

Materials:
DMC Embroidery floss No. 25: 646, 677, 741, 844, 988, 989, 3346 / No. 5: 989

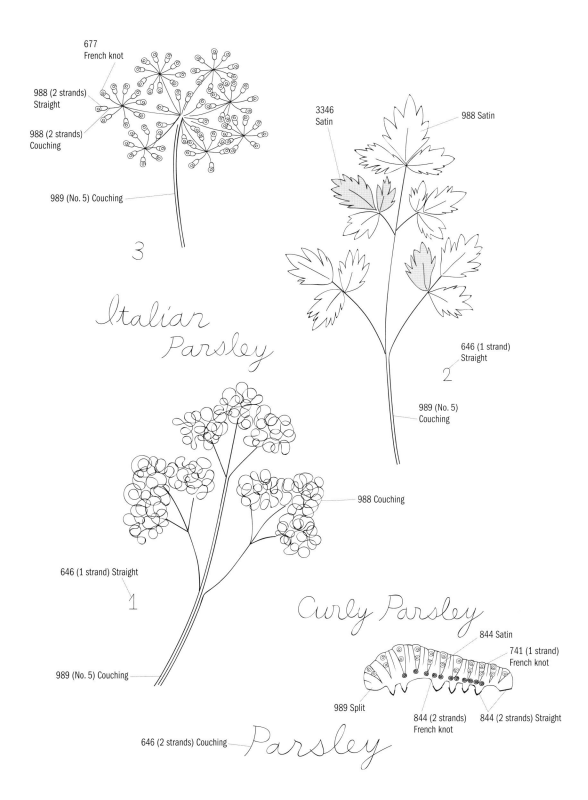

677
French knot

988 (2 strands)
Straight

988 (2 strands)
Couching

989 (No. 5) Couching

3

Italian Parsley

3346
Satin

988 Satin

646 (1 strand)
Straight

2

989 (No. 5)
Couching

988 Couching

646 (1 strand) Straight

1

989 (No. 5) Couching

Curly Parsley

844 Satin

741 (1 strand)
French knot

989 Split

844 (2 strands)
French knot

844 (2 strands) Straight

646 (2 strands) Couching *Parsley*

Materials:
DMC Embroidery floss No. 25: 155, 208, 320, 368, 646, 988, 3746, 3863 / No. 5: 368

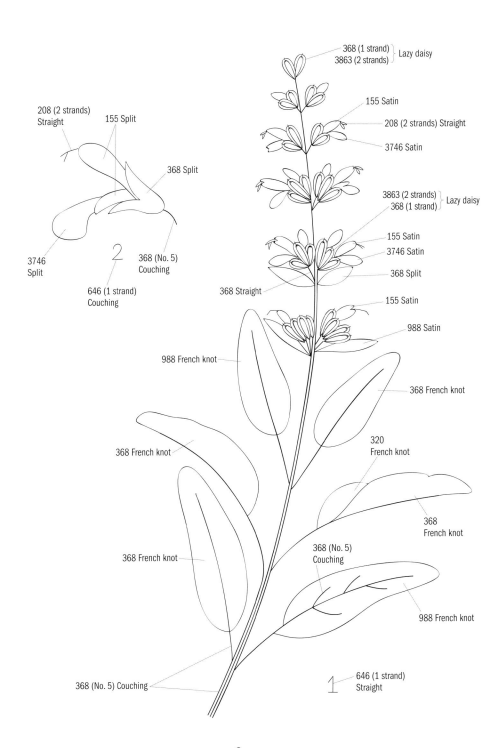

368 (1 strand)
3863 (2 strands) } Lazy daisy

155 Satin

208 (2 strands) Straight

3746 Satin

208 (2 strands)
Straight

155 Split

368 Split

3746
Split

368 (No. 5)
Couching

646 (1 strand)
Couching

3863 (2 strands)
368 (1 strand) } Lazy daisy

155 Satin

3746 Satin

368 Split

368 Straight

155 Satin

988 Satin

988 French knot

368 French knot

368 French knot

320
French knot

368
French knot

368 French knot

368 (No. 5)
Couching

988 French knot

368 (No. 5) Couching

646 (1 strand)
Straight

Sage

646 (2 strands) Couching

Materials:
DMC embroidery floss No. 25: 646, 729, 844, 902, 3023, 3348, 3712, 3722, 3803, ECRU

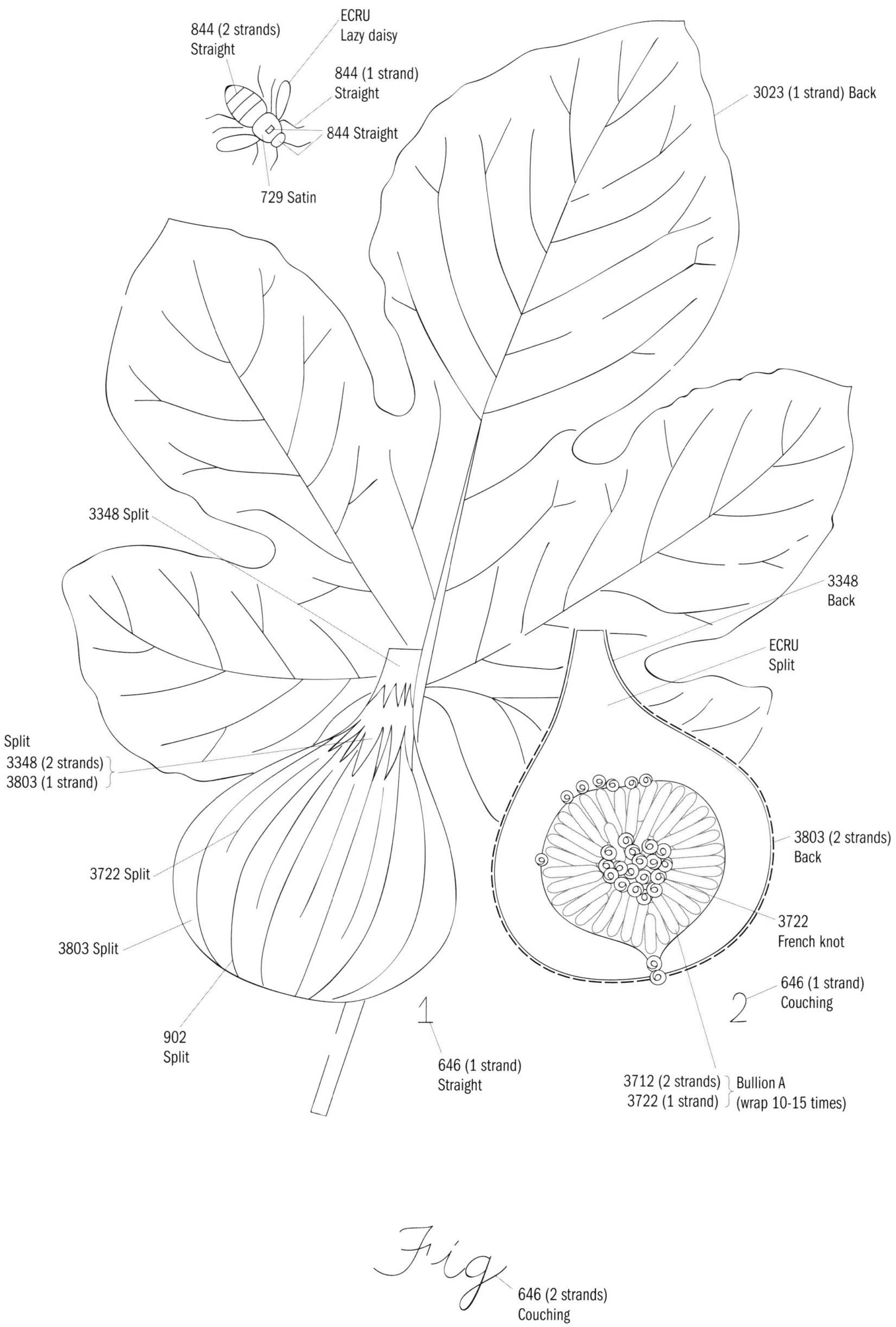

844 (2 strands)
Straight

ECRU
Lazy daisy

844 (1 strand)
Straight

844 Straight

729 Satin

3023 (1 strand) Back

3348 Split

3348
Back

ECRU
Split

Split
3348 (2 strands)
3803 (1 strand)

3722 Split

3803 (2 strands)
Back

3803 Split

3722
French knot

902
Split

646 (1 strand)
Couching

646 (1 strand)
Straight

3712 (2 strands) } Bullion A
3722 (1 strand) } (wrap 10-15 times)

1

2

Fig

646 (2 strands)
Couching

JUNEBERRY page 45

Materials:
DMC embroidery floss No. 25: 326, 646, 777, 840, 988, 3328, 3346, 3348, 3363, 3364, ECRU /
No. 5: 840

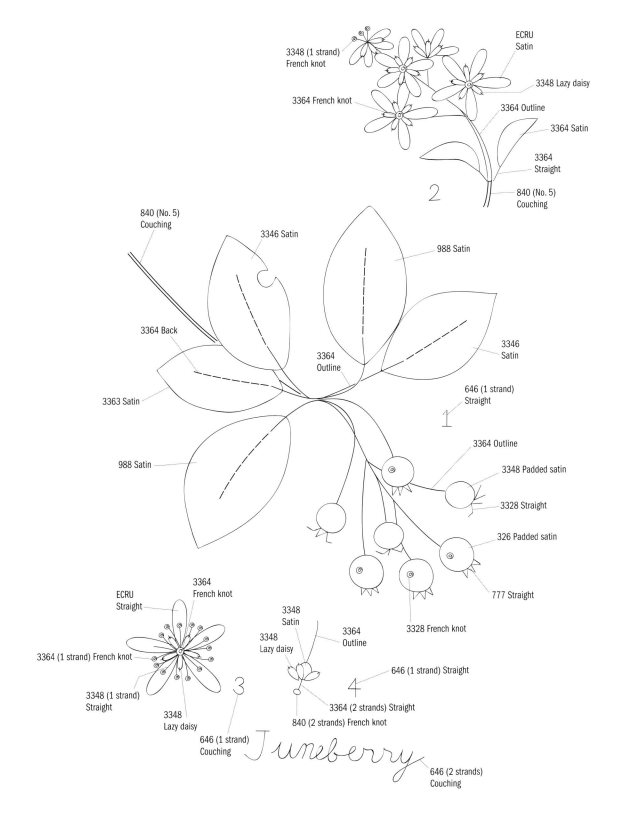

3348 (1 strand)
French knot

ECRU
Satin

3348 Lazy daisy

3364 French knot

3364 Outline

3364 Satin

3364
Straight

2

840 (No. 5)
Couching

840 (No. 5)
Couching

3346 Satin

988 Satin

3364 Back

3364
Outline

3346
Satin

3363 Satin

646 (1 strand)
Straight

988 Satin

3364 Outline

3348 Padded satin

3328 Straight

326 Padded satin

1

777 Straight

3328 French knot

ECRU
Straight

3364
French knot

3364 (1 strand) French knot

3348 (1 strand)
Straight

3348
Lazy daisy

3348
Satin

3348
Lazy daisy

3364
Outline

646 (1 strand) Straight

4

3

3364 (2 strands) Straight

840 (2 strands) French knot

646 (1 strand)
Couching

Juneberry

646 (2 strands)
Couching

91

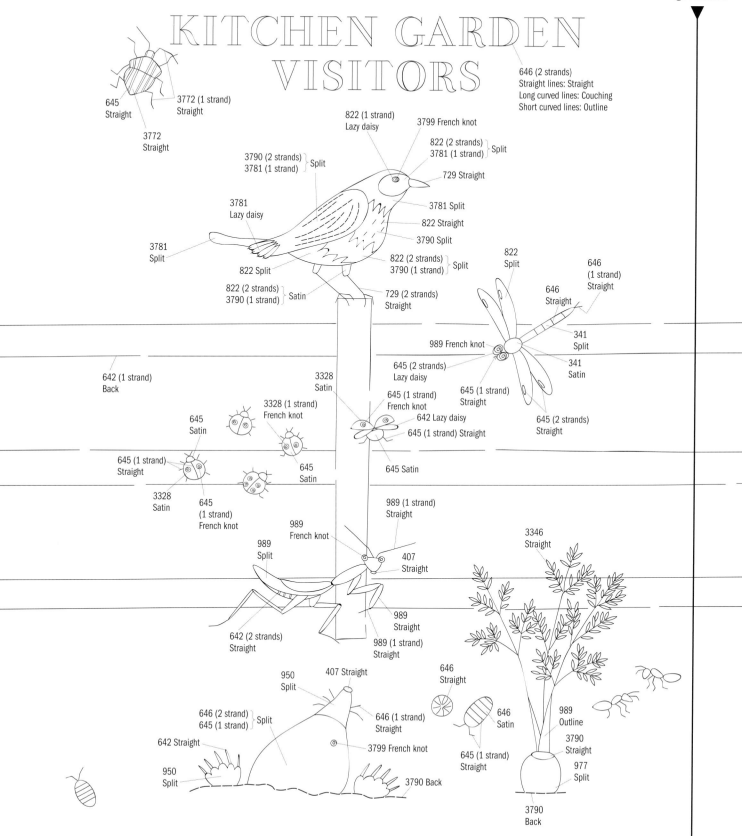

Align notches

645
Straight

3772 (1 strand)
Straight

3772
Straight

646 (2 strands)
Straight lines: Straight
Long curved lines: Couching
Short curved lines: Outline

822 (1 strand)
Lazy daisy

3799 French knot

822 (2 strands)
3781 (1 strand) } Split

3790 (2 strands)
3781 (1 strand) } Split

729 Straight

3781
Lazy daisy

3781 Split

822 Straight

3781
Split

3790 Split

822
Split

646
(1 strand)
Straight

646
Straight

822 (2 strands)
3790 (1 strand) } Split

822 Split

822 (2 strands)
3790 (1 strand) } Satin

729 (2 strands)
Straight

341
Split

341
Satin

642 (1 strand)
Back

3328
Satin

989 French knot

645 (2 strands)
Lazy daisy

3328 (1 strand)
French knot

645 (1 strand)
French knot

642 Lazy daisy

645 (1 strand) Straight

645 (1 strand)
Straight

645
Satin

645
Satin

645
Satin

645
Satin

3328
Satin

645
(1 strand)
French knot

989
Split

989
French knot

989 (1 strand)
Straight

407
Straight

3346
Straight

989
Straight

989 (1 strand)
Straight

989
Outline

642 (2 strands)
Straight

3790
Straight

977
Split

950
Split

407 Straight

646
Straight

646 (2 strand)
645 (1 strand) } Split

646 (1 strand)
Straight

646
Satin

642 Straight

3799 French knot

645 (1 strand)
Straight

950
Split

3790 Back

3790
Back

Align notches

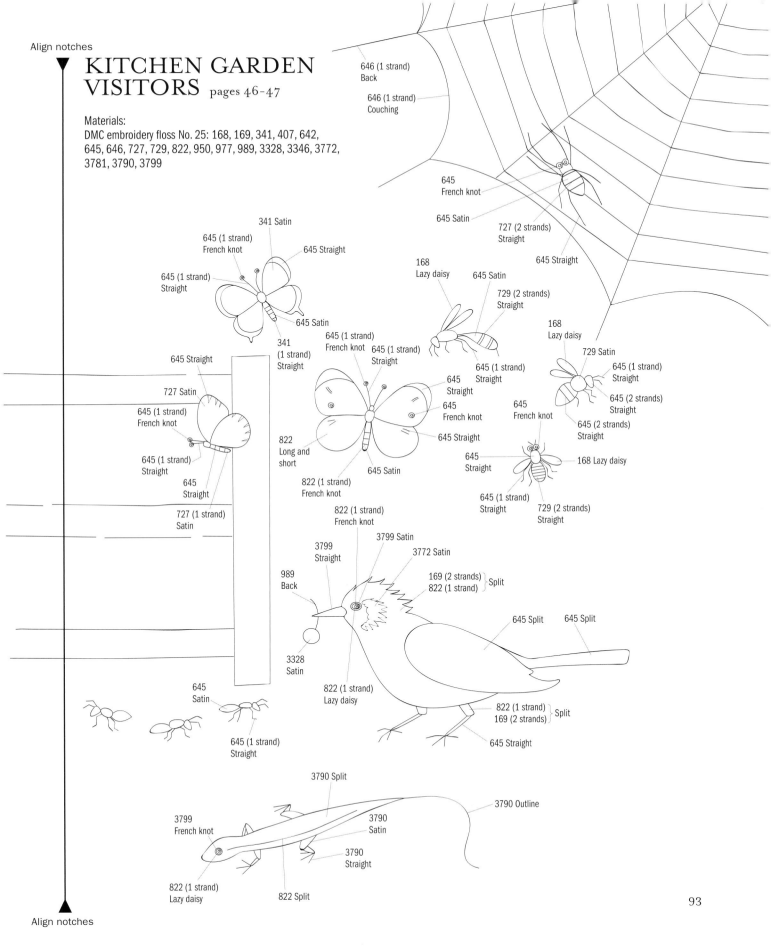

KITCHEN GARDEN VISITORS pages 46-47

Materials:
DMC embroidery floss No. 25: 168, 169, 341, 407, 642, 645, 646, 727, 729, 822, 950, 977, 989, 3328, 3346, 3772, 3781, 3790, 3799

646 (1 strand) Back
646 (1 strand) Couching

645 French knot
645 Satin
727 (2 strands) Straight
645 Straight

341 Satin
645 (1 strand) French knot
645 Straight
645 (1 strand) Straight
645 Satin
341 (1 strand) Straight

168 Lazy daisy
645 Satin
729 (2 strands) Straight
645 (1 strand) Straight

168 Lazy daisy
729 Satin
645 (1 strand) Straight
645 (2 strands) Straight
645 (2 strands) Straight

645 Straight
727 Satin
645 (1 strand) French knot
645 (1 strand) Straight
645 Straight
727 (1 strand) Satin

645 (1 strand) French knot
645 (1 strand) Straight
645 Straight
645 French knot
645 Straight
822 Long and short
822 (1 strand) French knot
645 Satin

645 French knot
645 Straight
645 (1 strand) Straight
729 (2 strands) Straight
168 Lazy daisy

822 (1 strand) French knot
3799 Straight
3799 Satin
3772 Satin
169 (2 strands) } Split
822 (1 strand) }
989 Back
645 Split
645 Split
3328 Satin
822 (1 strand) Lazy daisy
822 (1 strand) } Split
169 (2 strands) }
645 Straight

645 Satin
645 (1 strand) Straight

3790 Split
3790 Outline
3799 French knot
3790 Satin
3790 Straight
822 (1 strand) Lazy daisy
822 Split

Align notches

93

KITCHEN GARDEN FACTS

Komatsuna > page 33

· Common Names: Komatsuna, Japanese mustard spinach
· Scientific Name: Brassica rapa
· Place of Origin: Asia

Pumpkin and Squash > pages 34-35

· Common Names: Pumpkin, squash
· Scientific Name: Cucurbita moschata
· Place of Origin: Central and South America

Potatoes > page 36

· Common Name: Potato
· Scientific Name: Solanum tuberosum
· Place of Origin: South America

Onion > page 37

· Common Names: Common onion, bulb onion
· Scientific Name: Allium cepa
· Place of Origin: Central Asia

Chives > page 40

· Common Name: Chives
· Scientific Name: Allium schoenoprasum
· Place of Origin: Europe and Northern Asia

Marigold > page 41

· Common Name: Marigold
· Scientific Name: Tagetes patula
· Place of Origin: Mexico

Parsley > page 42

· Common Name: Parsley
· Scientific Name: Petroselinum crispum
· Place of Origin: Mediterranean coast

Sage > page 43

· Common Name: Sage
· Scientific Name: Salvia officinalis
· Place of Origin: Mediterranean coast and North Africa

Fig > page 44

· Common Name: Fig
· Scientific Name: Ficus carica
· Place of Origin: Arabian Peninsula

Juneberry > page 45

· Common Names: Juneberry, shadbush
· Scientific Name: Amelanchier canadensis
· Place of Origin: North Africa and North America

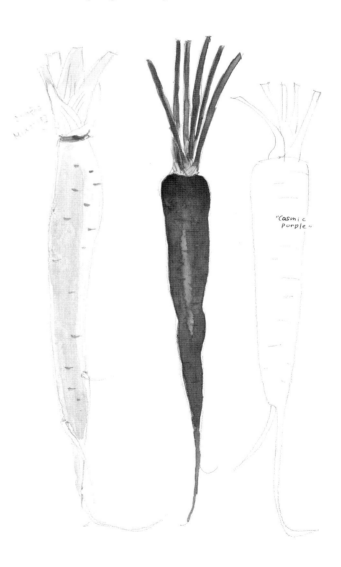

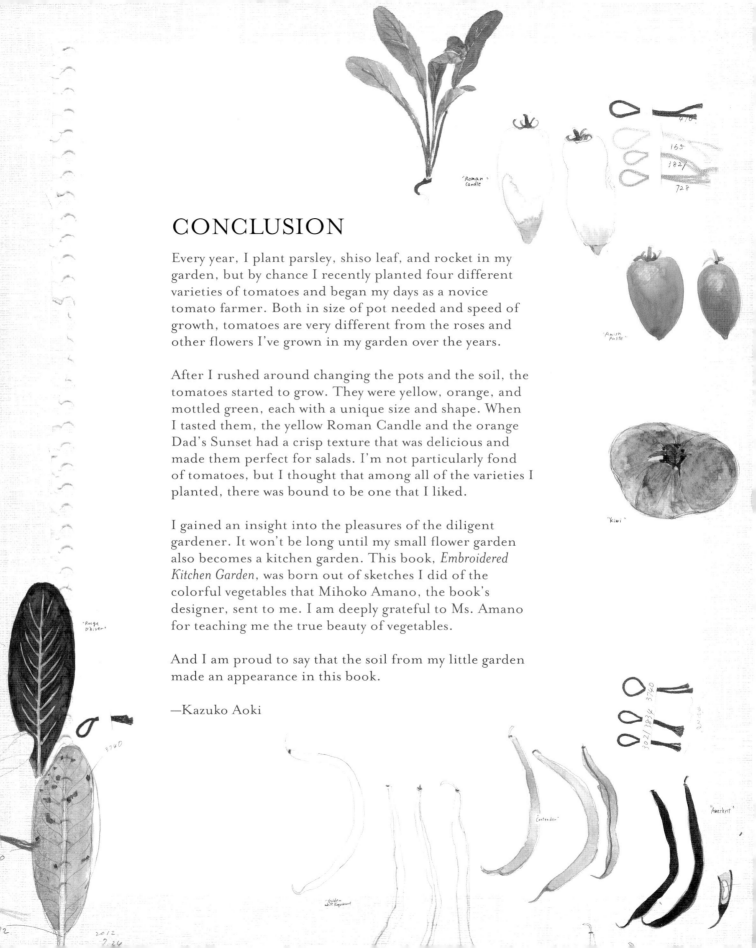

CONCLUSION

Every year, I plant parsley, shiso leaf, and rocket in my garden, but by chance I recently planted four different varieties of tomatoes and began my days as a novice tomato farmer. Both in size of pot needed and speed of growth, tomatoes are very different from the roses and other flowers I've grown in my garden over the years.

After I rushed around changing the pots and the soil, the tomatoes started to grow. They were yellow, orange, and mottled green, each with a unique size and shape. When I tasted them, the yellow Roman Candle and the orange Dad's Sunset had a crisp texture that was delicious and made them perfect for salads. I'm not particularly fond of tomatoes, but I thought that among all of the varieties I planted, there was bound to be one that I liked.

I gained an insight into the pleasures of the diligent gardener. It won't be long until my small flower garden also becomes a kitchen garden. This book, *Embroidered Kitchen Garden*, was born out of sketches I did of the colorful vegetables that Mihoko Amano, the book's designer, sent to me. I am deeply grateful to Ms. Amano for teaching me the true beauty of vegetables.

And I am proud to say that the soil from my little garden made an appearance in this book.

—Kazuko Aoki